"*There's Hope for Your Chu*... for anyone seeking to turn around a declining or plateaued church. McIntosh skillfully draws on his three decades of church consultations to forge a step-by-step strategy for restoring vitality to struggling churches. This book give you hope and will show you the way to revitalize your church."

Ed Stetzer, author of *Viral Churches*

"Gary McIntosh has written a down to earth practical book for those who look at the task of pastoring a church and don't know where to begin or what to do. *There's Hope for Your Church* is a coaching experience bound in the pages of a book. Gary McIntosh has consulted with over 1,000 churches, so he has seen most the problems, and there are very few difficulties in the church that he has not faced. Now Gary makes his wisdom available to help a pastor begin and carry through with a project of leading a church to become healthy and carry out the Great Commission."

Elmer Towns, cofounder of Liberty University

"I like this book because it helps me understand 'where' the church might find itself today and 'what' contributes to 'why' we have to wrestle with spiritual and pragmatic issues. But it doesn't leave me there. Gary McIntosh moves beyond mere analytical explanations and gives practical 'how-to's.' This book will take you from concept to completion. You'll not only read this book yourself but will want church leaders to read it as well."

Samuel R. Chand, author of *Cracking Your Church's Culture Code* (www.samchand.com)

"Once again McIntosh delivers a down-to-earth, practical book on how to turn around a troubled to dying church. Gary shares the turnaround wisdom he has gleaned for more than four decades of consulting with more than a 1,000 churches. This isn't armchair theology; it's the real deal."

"Once again Dr. Gary L. McIntosh's wealth of wisdom and experience shine a bright pathway for those wanting to see their churches healthy again. This book gives hope and practical insight for those doing the hard work of revitalization. I can't wait to get it into the hands of some of the pastors I work with!"

THERE'S
HOPE
FOR YOUR
CHURCH

THERE'S
HOPE
FOR YOUR
CHURCH

FIRST STEPS TO RESTORING
HEALTH AND GROWTH

GARY L. MCINTOSH

BakerBooks

a division of Baker Publishing Group
Grand Rapids, Michigan

Published by Baker Books
a division of Baker Publishing Group
P.O. Box 6287, Grand Rapids, MI 49516-6287
www.bakerbooks.com

Printed in the United States of America

Library of Congress Cataloging-in-Publication Data
McIntosh, Gary, 1947–
    There's hope for your church : first steps to restoring health and growth /
Gary L. McIntosh.
        p.   cm.
    Includes bibliographical references (p.   ).
    ISBN 978-0-8010-1406-2 (pbk.)
    1. Church renewal. I. Title.
BV600.3.M3537 2012
262.001'7—dc23   2011045088

Scripture quotations are from the New American Standard Bible®, copyright © 1960, 1962, 1963, 1968, 1971, 1972, 1973, 1975, 1977, 1995 by The Lockman Foundation. Used by permission.

The internet addresses, email addresses, and phone numbers in this book are accurate at the time of publication. They are provided as a resource. Baker Publishing Group does not endorse them or vouch for their content or permanence.

In keeping with biblical principles of creation stewardship, Baker Publishing Group advocates the responsible use of our natural resources. As a member of the Green Press Initiative, our company uses recycled paper when possible. The text paper of this book is composed in part of post-consumer waste.

To all revitalization leaders who know the pains and thrills of planting the seeds of change and reaping the fruit of new life in local churches

Contents

Acknowledgments

No book is a product of one person, even though most books have only one author. The reality is that a strong team works behind the scenes to bring an author's ideas to print. *There's Hope for Your Church* is no different, thus my appreciation and thanks go to executive editor Robert N. Hosack for ably steering my idea into manuscript status, to copyeditor Melinda Timmer for sharpening my writing in many ways, and to managing editor Mary Wenger for overseeing the entire process from beginning to end. Behind these people, of course, are a number of other individuals who worked diligently to bring this book to your hands. To them I also say thank you. It is a pleasure to work with all of you.

Preface

As you consider the future of your church, do you ever wish you could talk with a person who could answer your questions and point you in the right direction? As you consider the challenges and opportunities before your church, do you ever wish you had someone to coach you? Do you ever wish you had a mentor who could help you gain confidence in leading your church through a turnaround?

Well, allow this book to be your personal coach. It is the distillation of four decades of working as a coach and consultant with over one thousand churches, most of which were in need of revitalization. As you might expect, some did well and others did not, but lessons were learned from all of them—lessons I'll share with you in the pages of this book. I'll also share lessons discovered from pastoring two churches that were in desperate need of leadership. In one I faced traditional resistance to change and not much happened, but in the other, I was modestly successful. My experience in those two churches helps me to understand the dynamics and challenges that church leaders face in difficult situations. In addition to my position as professor of Christian ministry and leadership at Talbot School of Theology, Biola University in Southern California, I read numerous books, research studies, and doctoral dissertations that focus on various aspects of how to renew a church's vitality. So while I can't promise to know all the answers (I'm a learner as much as anyone), my hope is that *There's Hope for Your Church* will give you confidence and direction as you seek to revitalize your local church.

For simplicity, I've written in a down-to-earth, practical style. However, if you desire to explore church revitalization in more depth, an extensive reading list is included in appendix C. Support for the concepts taught in the following chapters can be found in these resources.

While I present a logical, step-by-step approach, revitalizing a church is messy. In real life, the following chapters often take place all at once, rather than step-by-step. Read the table of contents and feel free to jump into any chapter you feel might be helpful in light of your challenges. Fundamentally, however, it will be good for you to read the entire book straight through to gain a perspective of the entire process. *There's Hope for Your Church* is presented primarily to pastors, but anyone who is interested in helping his or her church move toward renewal will find the ideas helpful.

The church revitalization chart found at the beginning of each chapter will serve as a guide. The first step on the way to revitalizing any church is to see the possibilities. If you see potential for your church, start reading chapter 1 and keep going until you've thought about how each chapter figures into your church's ministry. Then when you finish reading the book, continue immersing yourself in the literature of revitalization (see appendix C). After you've spent time reading and reflecting on how to bring about renewal in a church, you'll begin to think and act differently. Hope begins in your own heart and mind, after which it seeps into your speech, practices, and body language. Your hope becomes a self-fulfilling prophecy. If you honestly believe there is hope for your church, your actions and attitudes will change.

So picture your church in the not-too-distant future. Imagine a gradually changing attitude reflecting a new sense of expectancy. Imagine people with a contagious enthusiasm for Christ and your church. Imagine classes pulsating with new life. Imagine a new spirit of hope in your church.

Is it possible? The answer . . . a resounding yes! It is possible. Indeed, God very much wants to see it happen. Do you believe that? I do. Can you see the possibilities? I can. Just think about it. There's hope for your church!

1

See the Potential

There are no hopeless situations; there are only people who have grown hopeless about them.

CLARE BOOTHE LUCE

Do you believe that?

I certainly do. If you want your church to experience fresh vitality, you must believe it too!

Unfortunately, many pastors and lay leaders engage church life with a certain lack of hope. Having begun with great hope for what God could do in their church, over the years they have become worn down by resistance, barriers, and circumstances. Many appear to have tried, as best they know how, to renew their church's vitality. Yet, after years of trying, struggling, and failing, they are discouraged. One of my friends expressed it this way: "Many local churches start with good intentions that are somehow lost amidst the fray.

17

Early advantages and opportunities slip through their fingers. Patterns of complacency and compromise emerge. *Slow death* goes to work with symptomless deception."[1] Consider, for example, the story of Pastor William Douglas.

One Pastor's Story

When Pastor Will accepted his appointment to Faith Evangelical Church, his heart literally raced with excitement. After talking one evening for an hour and a half with members of the pastoral search committee and hearing of their enthusiasm for his coming as their new pastor, he could not sleep. Tossing and turning throughout the night, he envisioned a great future for the church and, of course, for his own ministry. His heart was filled with hope for the future.

Members and attendees welcomed Will and his wife, Gail, with great fanfare. Expecting their first child, Will and Gail dreamed of a long ministry at Faith, perhaps even one that would last a lifetime. They fit the church well, matching the average age of the congregation and its middle-class values. Will's theology paralleled the church's viewpoint perfectly, and people showed evidence of a loving spirit. From any person's perspective, Will and Gail were right for the church and it for them.

After his first month of preaching, Will gathered the leaders of the church in a small classroom to plan the coming year together. Vacation Bible school, adult fellowship meetings, and holiday events were penciled onto a large calendar placed at the front of the room. All who participated in the planning seemed hopeful that the next year would be one of the best in the church's short, twenty-three-year history. Everyone shared openly and in prayer for the future of the church. The future looked promising.

Ministry flowed smoothly for the first three months as Will enjoyed the natural wave of congregational morale during what pastors call the honeymoon phase. However, a casual meeting with one of the church leaders during his thirteenth week caused Will to see a different reality.

"Will," Elder Lowe remarked, "I guess you know you were our last hope."

Reacting with a bit of surprise in his voice, Will asked, "What do you mean?"

"Well, I guess you should know that we had gone through nineteen candidates before we asked you to be our pastor," Elder Lowe revealed with a hint of embarrassment. "Each one turned us down for one reason or another. We finally decided we'd give it one last try, and if another candidate turned us down, we'd vote to close the church."

Shocked at this new information, Will simply sat at his desk in quiet thought. Elder Lowe finally broke the silence, declaring, "Pastor, you are our last hope. We've been on a slow decline for the last, oh, eight years or so. If you can't help us reach some new families, we still might need to close our doors."

Last hope? Will did not know what to say. He just thanked Elder Lowe for the information and excused himself by saying he had another appointment.

Will filed Elder Lowe's comment in the back of his mind and threw himself into his work for the next three months. "After all," Will ruminated, "I'm not the Savior of the church; Jesus is." His attempts to start a couple of new ministries were met with apathy. Church leaders never rejected his ideas outright but simply said, "That's fine, Pastor. Do what you want." Few people, however, ever volunteered to help. Eventually, Will determined to try some drastic measures to awaken the people. He suggested the church relocate to a new, growing area of town. This idea woke up the people all right, but just enough to rouse their anger. They rejected the idea through a congregational vote. He then turned to a fellow pastor at a sister church to discuss his situation. After several weeks, Will suggested to his church the possibility of a merger with their sister church. Several months of meetings, discussions, and shared worship services ensued, but in the end, the result was the same. When it came to a vote of the congregation, Will's idea was turned down. Two years of hard work left Will greatly discouraged and without hope. He resigned exactly two years to the day he had arrived.

Will's saga is not new. Going from hope to hopelessness is an old story that was first noted in the second and third chapters of the book of Revelation. Ephesus experienced fatigue and forgot its first love. Pergamum became careless about church discipline. Thyatira ignored internal conflict and refused to confront sin. Sardis lost passion for the future by resting on past accomplishments. Laodicea lost its influence due to its affluence. Five of the seven churches mentioned, 71 percent, faced difficulty, which is close to the 75 percent of churches that are at risk in North America today.

Roughly three-fourths of established churches in North America are either declining or on a long-term plateau. Such churches are ineffective at making disciples—at least new disciples—and function with a lack of fruitfulness and hope. Yet, as Clare Boothe Luce noted years ago, "There are no hopeless situations; there are only people who have grown hopeless about them."

One of the most revealing illustrations of Luce's statement is found in the research of Viktor Frankl. While a prisoner in the Auschwitz concentration camp, he watched people living and dying daily and later published his observations in *Man's Search for Meaning.* He observed that people simply die when they have no hope. If people allow apathy to set in, if they have no purpose, and if they see no meaning in life, they give up. But if they have hope, if they lean toward the positive in life, and if they have a purpose, they live.

While Frankl's focus was on individual people, I've noted that churches act like individual people. Local churches have traits, personalities, and attitudes. Just like people, churches that have no purpose allow apathy to set in. They lose hope and die. The good news is churches that see problems as opportunities, set goals, and move into the future with hope, live! There's hope for your church! Do you believe that? If you do, your church is likely to thrive. As Henry Ford reportedly remarked, "Whether you think you can or can't, you're right."

Reasons for Hope

There's hope for your church! Do you believe that? I do. Why am I so hopeful? Let me give you three reasons (there are more, but these will suffice for now). First, God wants your church to grow. The first mention of the church in the Bible contains God's promise that his church will grow: "I also say to you that you are Peter, and upon this rock I will build My church; and the gates of Hades will not overpower it" (Matt. 16:18). The concept of "church" in this passage contains the seeds of both the universal church and local churches. Today there are approximately two billion Christians in the world. Compared to the small band of believers that met together in the upper room in Acts 1, the worldwide church makes it clear that Christ's church has grown. He has kept his promise. These two billion people meet in local gatherings called churches. They may meet secretly in a home in China, out in the open under a tree in Africa, or in a modern, air-conditioned building in Canada, but they gather in communities of faith to worship, pray, and learn. Thus, as local churches grow, the universal church grows; as the universal church grows, local churches grow. According to Christ, even the gates of Hades will not stop the advance of his church. Since your church is part of God's plan, there is hope for your church in God's promise to build his church.

God wants your church to be fruitful and multiply. Acts 12:24 reports that "the word of the Lord continued to grow and to be multiplied." This report regarding the early church brought back powerful memories to the disciples. The words

21

fruitful and multiply imply an expectation of numerical growth of new disciples and churches. Tracing the phrase in the Old Testament confirms this.

The phrase *fruitful and multiply* goes all the way back to the creation of man and woman in Genesis 1:28, where God said, "Be fruitful and multiply, and fill the earth." Over the ensuing years, Adam and Eve obeyed this command, and the earth was gradually filled with people. Unfortunately, the sin of man (Gen. 6) brought forth God's judgment through the flood (Gen. 7–8). Yet, after Noah and his sons left the ark, God reiterated his command, "Be fruitful and multiply, and fill the earth" (Gen. 9:1). God commanded Noah and his sons to produce offspring and to spread across the face of the earth. Later, God used the same two words in his promise to multiply the seed of Abraham (Gen. 17:6; 22:17), a promise God restated to Jacob in Genesis 35:11: "I am God almighty; be fruitful and multiply; a nation and a company of nations shall come from you." Once again, there is no doubt that this promise included an expectation that the nation of Israel would grow numerically. So it is no surprise when the first chapter of Exodus states, "But the sons of Israel were fruitful and increased greatly, and multiplied, and became exceedingly mighty, so that the land was filled with them" (1:7). The people of Israel understood that numerical growth of their nation was tied directly to their obedience. God promised Israel that if they kept his commands, "I will turn toward you and make you fruitful and multiply you" (Lev. 26:9).

When Luke used the words *fruitful and multiply* in Acts 12:24, the early disciples understood the implication: churches are to grow and multiply across the world as new believers accept the gospel of salvation in Jesus Christ. Even the apostle Paul used a similar phrase when he described the expansion of the Christian faith in the world. Speaking about the spread of the gospel, he wrote, "Just as in all the world also it is constantly *bearing fruit and increasing*" (Col. 1:6, emphasis added). Wouldn't you like to see your church constantly bearing fruit and increasing? It can happen. God expects it. There is hope for your church, just as there is for all churches that obediently follow God's commands.

Second, God revitalizes and restores people, nations, and churches that have lost spiritual energy. The Old Testament records several cycles of rebellion, repentance, and restoration in the book of Judges. Whenever the nation rebelled and then repented, God raised up a new leader called a judge—Othniel, Ehud, Deborah, Gideon, Jephthah, Samson, etc.—who brought restoration to the nation. Chronicles records several revivals under King Asa (2 Chron. 14–16), King Jehoshaphat (2 Chron. 20), King Hezekiah (2 Chron. 30), and King Josiah (2 Chron. 34). The New Testament records beautiful pictures of restoration, such as the return of the prodigal son in Luke 15 and the call to the churches in Revelation: "He who has an ear, let him hear what the Spirit says to the churches" (Rev. 2:7, 11, 17, 29; 3:6, 13, 22). The implication in Revelation is that God will restore churches that hear and repent. The bottom line is that there is hope for your church! God desires to renew your church and will do so if the people listen and repent (more about this later on).

Third, God is revitalizing churches right now. For the last three decades, I've observed churches throughout the United States and Canada being renewed and revitalized. While there is not room here to share all the details, here is one church's story.

Crestline Community Church was in financial trouble following the resignation of its fourth pastor in less than five years. While church members often commented that they were the friendliest church in town, the facts proved otherwise. Few visitors bothered to come through the doors of the church, and during the five years of turmoil, the church had declined 13 percent. The church was in trouble, and everyone knew it, even if they didn't speak about it openly.

In a last-ditch effort to turn the church around, a call was issued to Pastor Neal Westman. He had seven years of church-planting experience, and the church members hoped he could bring the necessary tools to restore the health and vitality of their church. In a letter to Pastor Westman, the church board told him they were desperate and were ready to do what was needed to attract and keep younger families.

Pastor Westman hit the ground running, and the congregation allowed him to make several significant changes during his first year. Facilities were refurbished, a new children's ministry was started, advertising was sent to the surrounding community, a new adult class was added, an evangelism training course was introduced, and a building fund was started with a small deposit of one hundred dollars. Over the next year, morale gradually increased as attendance rose 52 percent. Within five years, the church grew from 52 people to a high of 145. By the time Pastor Westman left the church ten years later, worship attendance was averaging 210 people in two worship services.

This too is an old story. God is in the practice of restoring, renewing, and revitalizing people *and* churches, if they are willing to follow him and pay the price to see it happen. There is hope for your church!

Bringing It Home

1. Is there hope for your church? Why do you think this?

2. Which of the reasons for hope mentioned in this chapter do you find most appealing? Which do you question?

3. What other reasons for hope can you think of that were not noted in this chapter?

4. If your church were willing to change, what might the potential be for the future? Be specific and paint a picture of what you see for your church in the next five to ten years.

2

Commit to Lead

If you're gonna stand around here, you've got to keep movin'.

COMMENT BY A POLICEMAN
TO PEOPLE STANDING ON A CORNER

An old adage assures us that "a new broom sweeps clean." If you are a church leader exploring the potential of revitalizing your church, you are the new broom. In your efforts to bring fresh energy into your church, you will be attempting to "sweep your church clean," to shake things up, to get the church moving, to implement changes.

Your passion is admirable, but you will be faced with unseen hazards that must be removed or avoided before you can proceed. How do you revitalize your church without losing your sanity? Or, in the case of a pastor, your job?

A great deal of research during the last sixty

years has focused on the issue of church revitalization. In the 1950s and 1960s, the Church Renewal Movement stressed the importance of spiritual renewal, focusing on small group Bible study and prayer. The following decades of the 1970s and 1980s saw the emergence of the Church Growth Movement with its emphasis on evangelism and strategic planning. An emphasis on church health gained momentum in the 1990s, returning to an inward look similar to the Church Renewal Movement's emphasis on spiritual dynamics. That emphasis merged with the spiritual formation interest found in numerous churches. More recently, the last two decades have stressed missional outreach as a means of revitalizing local churches. In all the research completed throughout these years, one aspect stands out: the importance of leadership, especially pastoral leadership. In order for a church to be revitalized, the pastor is the key.

However, it must be a particular kind of leadership. Revitalization consultant Ken Priddy[1] points out that there are two types of pastors: a revitalization pastor and a revitalization leader. Important differences make one an effective turnaround leader, while the other sees much less success.

According to Priddy's analysis, revitalization pastors see the church as their client. This makes sense, since most pastors are called or appointed by a church committee, report to a church board, and receive a salary from the church. As a result, both the church and the pastor view the pastor as an employee of the church. Thus, pastors feel they must do what the church desires, and the process of revitalization is seen as gaining a consensus among the church members to take the church where it wants to go. Unfortunately, consensus building takes a good deal of time, and implementing changes in such a situation is extremely difficult. Add to this the desire of most pastors to receive affirmation from the congregation, and it is easy to see that doing anything contrary to what the church wants brings pain rather than joy. The bottom line is that revitalization pastors rarely see a church turned around, even if they think the church needs to change.

In contrast, some pastors are revitalization leaders. While they work for the church, report to a board, and receive a salary, such pastors see God as their client. Therefore, they do what God desires rather than what church members desire. Rather than being an employee of the church, revitalization leaders believe they are called by God and must lead the church where God wants it to go. Thus, they see the process of revitalization as taking the church where it doesn't want to go but needs to go. Revitalization leaders expect to encounter resistance and are willing to lead without affirmation and often with pain.

Terry Walling, a leader who specializes in helping churches refocus their ministry, puts it like this: "For churches to transition into a new era of ministry, courageous, godly leadership is paramount."[2]

CASE STUDY 1
Pastor or Leader

"I never signed up for this," Pastor Sam Holland thought quietly. He would never say such a thing to others, well, maybe to his wife, but not to any worshipers at his church. Nevertheless, he honestly thought ministry would be smoother.

He just wanted to preach to, love, and care for the people at West Island Church. He hoped that by doing so his church members would show respect and love in return. Things had gone well for almost two years, but now he sensed an increasing dissatisfaction with his leadership from the church family.

He knew the church was in need of repair. In particular, the sanctuary needed upgrading to be attractive to newcomers. When he suggested that seating in the sanctuary could be improved by taking out the old pews and replacing them with movable seating, people criticized him publicly. A few key leaders even threatened to leave if the remodeling idea went forward. Some of them recalled with emotion how they had raised the money to purchase the pews from a mortuary that had closed. The brass plates attached to the ends of the pews bore their names and the names of their friends who were now gone.

The problem got even worse when others threatened to leave if the church didn't move forward on the project. One of the newer members told Pastor Holland, "If we don't remodel the sanctuary, it'll be a vote for no growth. My family and I will be leaving if we don't move forward on this new vision."

Pastor Holland agonized over the fact that people were disagreeing on such a small matter. At least it was small from his viewpoint. Finally, rather than causing the church and himself so much pain, Pastor Holland decided to drop the idea and work for peace among the parties. He hoped that neither group would leave the church. "After all," he mused, "we should be able to get along."

Analysis:

- Is Pastor Holland a revitalization pastor or a revitalization leader? What indicators can you point to that support your view?
- What seems to be the major obstacle that Pastor Holland is struggling with in his own heart?
- How difficult is it going to be for Pastor Holland to revitalize West Island Church? What makes you think that way?

Revitalization Leaders

Leaders who are willing to accept the challenge of guiding a church toward fresh health and vitality exhibit the following characteristics.

The right personality.

Studies of pastors who have led a church to renewed and sustained growth consistently show that there is a distinct personality type of a revitalization leader. According to the familiar DISC personality profile, a revitalization leader overwhelmingly falls into either the D or the I personality type.

The DISC personality profile is built on the axis of two continuums. The first continuum identifies people as either people-oriented or task-oriented, while the second continuum separates people into response-oriented and action-oriented. Put together, the two continuums look like figure 1.

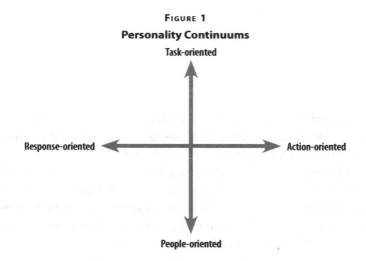

FIGURE 1
Personality Continuums

Basically, people tend to focus on either completing a task or taking care of people, and they tend to take action to accomplish a project or to respond by helping others complete a project. The DISC personality profile is built on a complex series of studies, but answering the two questions below can give you an indication of your personality type. Read the following two questions and circle the letters on figure 2 that correspond to your answers.

Question 1: When working with a group of people on a project, are you motivated mostly by (a) finishing the task or (b) fellowshiping with the workers?

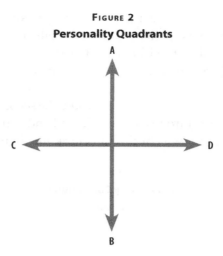

FIGURE 2

Personality Quadrants

Question 2: When you see a job that needs to be done, do you (c) wait until others start doing it and then help them or (d) jump in and begin to do it yourself?

The two continuums produce four quadrants. The quadrant between the two letters you circled is generally your personality type.[3] Using the DISC descriptions, the four personality types are Dominance, Influence, Supportive, and Conscientious. This is illustrated in figure 3.

People who have a D personality are dominant, often leading in a somewhat demanding way. D's are typically decisive and directive in their leadership style. Their tendencies include getting results, creating action, making fast decisions, solving problems, and taking charge.

Like a D leader, the I leader is also action-oriented but seeks to influence those around them to move forward rather than demanding they do so. I's typically take initiative and influence people through an entertaining style of communication. Their tendencies include making a good impression, articulating vision, generating enthusiasm, entertaining people, and creating a positive environment.

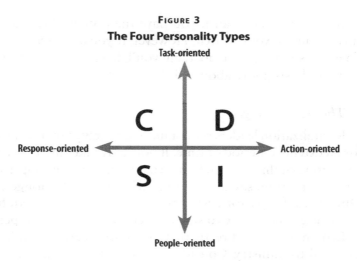

FIGURE 3

The Four Personality Types

The S leader likes to encourage and care for others. S's typically are steady and supportive in their personality style. They enjoy working with others to complete a task. Their tendencies include supporting others, listening well, displaying loyalty, remaining patient, and calming others.

The C leader is concerned with the details surrounding a project. C's are highly conscientious about getting work done and desire that things be done correctly. Their tendencies include attention to detail, critical thinking, doing things correctly, complying with authority, and promoting quality.

Speaking about pastoral leadership, C. Peter Wagner noted years ago, "Some pastors are take-charge people, and some never bring themselves to take charge."[4] Revitalizing a church requires leaders to take charge rather than waiting for someone else to begin. Thus, revitalization leaders tend to be either a D or an I personality type. God, of course, can use anyone, and he does at times use people with an S or a C personality to revitalize a church. However, studies completed on pastors who have successfully revitalized a church demonstrate that such pastors are invariably either a D or an I.[5]

If you are a D or an I, you have the potential to lead a turnaround in your church. However, if you are an S or a C, do not despair. You can do it, but you'll have to build a strong team to do so (more about this in chap. 6).

The right timing.

Revitalization leaders are committed to stay at their church for an extended period of time. It normally takes five to seven years to revitalize a church in a city. It takes much longer in a rural situation, say, about ten to fifteen years (or longer!). Obviously, if a pastor desires to see a church revitalized, he or she is going to have to stay long enough to see it happen.

Length of stay is directly tied to a pastor's understanding of a call to ministry. Considering the difficulties and challenges faced in turning a church around, a pastor must be committed to a clear call of God. A pastor's call provides the assurance that he is in the right place at the right time.

Our church did not begin to move forward until the congregation believed I had made a commitment to stay with them.

Pastor David F. Nixon

Howard Sugden and Warren Wiersbe, writing in *Confident Pastoral Leadership*, assert, "The work of the ministry is too demanding and difficult for a man to enter it without a sense of divine calling. Men enter and then leave the ministry usually because they lack a sense of divine urgency."[6] This is certainly accurate of revitalization leaders. After extensive research on the personality traits of effective revitalization leaders, Robert Thomas concluded that revitalization ministry "is extremely draining and exacts a toll on the pastor and his family. A person must be certain of a 'call' from God before embarking upon this task."[7]

In my interviews with pastors, I've found that revitalization leaders are certain about two aspects of their call. First, they are certain that God has called them to make their living from the gospel; that is, they are sure God wants them in the ministry and not some other field of work. Second, they are certain that God has placed them in their current ministry location; that is, they are not looking over the fence at another ministry position. Revitalization leaders do not question either of these two aspects. Rather, they move forward in confidence that they are where God wants them to be.

One of the reasons most pastors are not successful at bringing about revitalization is that they don't stay long enough. John Maxwell illustrates the impact of staying at a church in his "Five Levels of Leadership."[8] According to Maxwell, during the first two years of a pastor's ministry in a church, he or she leads from positional authority. I remember a conversation with my grandmother years ago. I had been critical of my teachers in school, and my grandmother told me, "Gary, no matter what your teachers are like, you must still respect them." Like others, I soon learned that it is proper to follow and respect others just because they have a certain position. Thus, no matter our feelings, we honor our teacher, the policeman who pulls us over for a traffic violation, and the pastor of our church. Yet, positional leadership is just the beginning, and it is not a very strong platform from which to lead a church toward revitalization.

As pastors build solid relationships in the first two years of ministry, people begin to follow them because they are likable. Maxwell calls this second level of leadership leading by permission—the people like you and give you permission to lead them. This is a much stronger form of leadership than positional leadership because it moves beyond the initial platform of respect to that of relationship. This level of leadership lasts about another two years for most pastors.

During the fourth to the seventh years, a pastor transitions onto a more powerful level of leadership referred to as leading by production. Ministries and programs that were put into place during the first four years begin to bear fruit by the seventh year. Good ideas planted in the first few years sprout good results in the fourth to the seventh years, leading to a new level of leadership. When people see that your ideas have borne fruit, they start to follow you because they trust your leadership skills. This level of leadership then slowly evolves into a new level of leadership known as leading by personal development.

The fourth level of leadership—personal development—comes about when people's lives are changed. Over the years, a pastor contributes to people's lives through preaching, mentoring, and caring. Long days spent with people at the hospital, evening counseling sessions with couples, and hours of mentoring future leaders begin to pay dividends as people recognize how they've grown from your investment in their lives. Gradually, between years seven and fifteen, a pastor notices that people are following at a new level. An investment into members' lives is returned in a new level of trust.

The few pastors who stay fifteen years or longer discover an even higher level of leadership authority called leading by personhood. A pastor who ministers effectively in a church for fifteen years or more has baptized, counseled, and taught many people. In a real way, church members, worshipers, and even people in the larger community around the church esteem such pastors highly. People follow because of who the pastor is as a person. Unfortunately, few pastors in our day reach this level of leadership authority.

The problem related to revitalizing a church is that the average tenure of a pastor is less than four years (my observation is that senior or solo pastors in the United States stay in a church an average of 3.8 years). If my observation is correct, some 90 percent of pastors don't make it past the four-year mark in a local church. What typically takes place is that a conflict of some sort arises in the third or fourth year of a pastor's ministry in a congregation. Perhaps church members and leaders begin to understand the impact on the church of what the pastor desires to do and begin to resist changes. For example, the people may say they want to grow. However, when people begin to realize growth means changing the worship style, or a host of other possible changes, they resist the idea. The congregation votes against any changes with their money, time, attendance, and, if a congregational meeting is needed, their actual votes. The pastor sees this resistance as an unwillingness to follow his leadership and leaves the church, only to repeat the process in another church.

The desire to give up and move on is intense. A ministry friend, Chris Conrad, has written about the desire to leave as follows:

> I've had the privilege of spending most of my life in what most would call "successful ministry situations." I'm humbled by the fact that I've had the privilege of being used by God to lead "successful," high-paced, life-changing ministry. I know what it's like to feel like I'm going Mach 2 above the desert floor, having the time of my life as God pours out more blessing than we ever deserve. To him be the praise!
>
> I also know what it's like to crawl in the sand on that very same desert floor. To have sand in your hair, in your mouth, in your eyes . . . longing, pleading for a drink of refreshing ministry . . . but nothing comes. And all you can hear are the sounds of planes overhead as they break the sound barrier with their fast-paced, awe-inspiring, high-profile ministries.
>
> That's what a tough ministry challenge feels like. Crawling in the sand of the desert floor while others fly high overhead.
>
> The temptation to give up is intense. So is the temptation to develop "ministry envy." To look at others who, for whatever reason, have been given easier ministry assignments and ask, "What's up with this, God?"[9]

I once attended the retirement banquet for a pastor who had been in pastoral ministry forty years. When it came time for him to say a few closing words, he said, "I'm proud to say I've pastored ten churches in my forty years." The truth was he had not had forty years of ministry but rather four years of ministry repeated ten times! That length of tenure will never lead to revitalized churches. The great majority of churches will not be revitalized unless pastors commit to staying at least seven years. The bottom line is that revitalization leaders stay.

It is possible, however, for pastors to stay too long. In my experience, if a church has not experienced revitalization within ten to twelve years of a pastor's tenure, it is not going to happen. Many pastors have a vision capacity for about ten years in a single church. Some, of course, can lead a church for twenty years, and a few thirty to forty years. Yet, the average pastor's ministry tends to lose momentum after ten years. Why is this so? The average pastor usually has the knowledge, skill, and energy to maintain a ten-year ministry. After ten years, many pastors frankly do not know what to do. The original vision they had for the church has most likely been accomplished, and now the church flounders, searching for a new direction. Some pastors are able to reenvision their life and ministry for another ten years in the same church, but some cannot and find it best to move to another ministry. My advice is that if you have been in your church for less than seven years, you need to stay longer; if you've been there ten or twelve years, you must either capture a new vision for the next ten years or leave for a different ministry.

The right action.

Revitalization leaders are proactive rather than reactive. This is one of the reasons D's and I's are able to help revitalize a church when S's and C's have more difficulty. D's and I's are proactive, while S's and C's are reactive. Revitalization leaders do not wait for a consensus but take control and set direction. They take advantage of the honeymoon phase, realizing there is no time to waste. Observation shows that growth and revitalization happen faster rather than slower in a majority of churches. For example, one study of twenty revitalization leaders discovered that each was able to see renewal in growth between six months and three years of becoming the pastor. However, Robert Thomas reminds us, "Although rapid preplanned change is possible, many years of persistence are required to keep it in place."[10]

While a few churches take longer, some up to ten years, to turn around, in most situations the longer it takes, the more difficult it becomes. Long turnarounds lose momentum, people become discouraged, and leaders leave before true revitalization can happen. The exact speed of a turnaround is controlled by numerous variables. Progress, however, must be made even if slowly at first. Remember the law of the snake pit: if you ever find yourself in a pit full of snakes, keep moving but don't make any sudden jerks.

The right attitude.

One of the movies I remember watching as a child was about the fabled character Ulysses. In one scene, the enemy captured Ulysses and tied him between two teams of horses. The enemy commander ordered the horses to be whipped in an effort to tear Ulysses apart. Of course, in the movie, Ulysses had the strength to hold both teams of horses together, even though it was painful to do so.

Effective revitalization leaders are much like Ulysses in that they have to hold on to the old church while simultaneously building the new one. They have to minister to the former people while assimilating new people. They must work from the left, casting vision and hope, while working from the right, answering questions and

> *Leadership calls for suffering and struggle.*
> JIM COLLINS

bearing criticism. At times a revitalization leader will feel like Ulysses holding two teams of horses.

Leadership coach Sam Chand says, "The growth of a church is in direct proportion to a leader's willingness to suffer pain."[11] Revitalization leaders are willing to suffer the pain of criticism, people leaving the church, misunderstood motives, and a host of other occurrences. When I was going through a painful time of leadership some years ago, a friend told me, "If you are succeeding without suffering, someone has suffered before you. If you are suffering without succeeding, someone will succeed after you." I've since found those words to be true. No church is revitalized without someone suffering. If you are willing to suffer the pain, your church can be revitalized. If you are unwilling to suffer pain, the church cannot be revitalized. This is why it takes a revitalization leader rather than a revitalization pastor. Revitalization pastors want to lead with affirmation and joy, which never happens in a turnaround situation. Only revitalization leaders are willing to suffer the pain of a turnaround.

The right focus.

To a great extent, a fruitful ministry hinges on the heart of the pastor. If a church is to capture the heart of its community, Christ must first capture the heart of the pastor. Revitalization leaders live the mission. Leading a church through a period of revitalization takes a great toll on a pastor's emotional well-being. Remaining whole emotionally, spiritually, and physically is a fundamental necessity for those leading churches in fresh directions. Spiritual disciplines of prayer, rest, and quietness are prerequisites for lasting spiritual health. Pastors leading a church in revitalization will find their emotional lives taxed to the limit. Quiet reflection and trust in God will sustain the revitalization leader through times of discouragement and suffering.

> I know the price of success: dedication, hard work, and an unremitting devotion to the things you want to see happen.
> FRANK LLOYD WRIGHT

Bringing It Home

1. Do you see yourself as a revitalization pastor or a revitalization leader? How do you know?

2. According to the DISC profile, are you a D, I, S, or C? What does this imply about your ability to lead your church toward revitalization?

3. How long have you been at your church? What does this say about your ability to lead? Are you willing to remain at your church long enough to see revitalization become a reality?

4. What is your reaction to the statement, "The growth of a church is in direct proportion to a leader's willingness to suffer pain"?

3

Assess the Situation

You need to remove the fog.
DONALD A. McGAVRAN

Do you know the danger signs that could spell disaster for your church? In our fast-changing environment, disaster happens for a number of reasons. Sometimes it occurs when church leaders take their eyes off what the church is all about. Leaders of healthy, growing churches constantly ask two critical questions: What is our purpose? How are we doing? At other times, disaster takes place because leaders place their heads in the proverbial sand and refuse to acknowledge any problems. Still, in many cases, disaster creeps up on a church slowly, appearing to surprise even the most ardent church observer.

Signs of Trouble

No church needs to be taken by surprise. There are obvious signs of trouble if church leaders

41

will take the time to look. Unfortunately, assessing a church's situation is often not done. The reason? Pastors and other church leaders may find assessment uncomfortable. They may lack the patience to peer into the present situation, or they may not know what to assess. I believe an evaluation of a church's current situation is healthy, and it can be an enjoyable experience.

What follows are eight signs of trouble that may signal a need for revitalization in your church. Revitalization leaders take the time to evaluate their church in light of these signs.

Low morale.

It is surprising how quickly one notices the atmosphere or environment of a church after walking into the lobby on a Sunday morning. When visiting churches, I've experienced spans of emotion from happiness, celebration, and excitement to discouragement, hopelessness, and despair. People may feel they are disguising their true feelings from guests, but visitors can sense the true atmosphere within a few minutes of walking into the church building.

If you are sensitive to the atmosphere, you can tell how a church is doing. For example, how do you know if the people at a church are unhappy? They do not smile. How do you know if the people at a church are happy? They smile. So ask yourself if the people in your church are happy or unhappy. Do they smile or frown? Is there laughter or sadness? You can tell a lot about a church just by reading facial expressions. Are people avoiding each other? Avoiding you? Scowling?

Downward momentum.

I'm sure you've observed what happens when you fill a sink full of water and then pull the plug, allowing the water to drain out of the basin. As the water drains, a circular motion develops similar to a small tornado that gradually pulls the remaining water down the drain. A similar action is often seen in churches that are losing worshipers. The loss of people creates a downward force that results in a loss of programs, classes, and finances. This action actually has a name—cutback syndrome—that refers to the cutbacks that take place as resources dwindle. The more cutbacks a church makes, the less impact it has, and a momentum develops that pulls the church ever more downward.

Churches that show a decline or plateau lasting three or more years are churches at risk. Decline or plateauing is undesirable, as it translates into less disciples, resources, potential, and effectiveness. What has happened in the last three years of any church is very likely a predictor of what's going to happen in the next three years—unless something is done to change the course of the church's direction. However, if a church has been in decline for a decade or more, it may be a sign that it's time to close the church.[1]

Survival mode.

People who have spent years or even just a few months in a pressure-cooker atmosphere will be discouraged. They may even be angry with God, feeling that he has let them down. Lost dreams, threatened security, and feeling beat up not only result in lower morale but also produce a defensive attitude among the congregation. Leaders take a defensive position to protect themselves from additional hurt and danger. New ways of doing things and creative solutions are resisted. Thoughts turn to protecting what is left, resulting in a survival mode.

Passive attitudes.

One of the major challenges in declining and plateaued churches is recruiting new workers. Indeed, this may be the number one challenge facing pastors and leaders. Closely related are a lack of financial giving and poor attendance at worship services. Each of these is an indication of passive attitudes among the congregation. It's a clear sign of trouble when people have a wait-and-see attitude. Attempts to recruit new people into every area of church ministry meet with a so-so response. Hedging of bets becomes the norm. Perhaps members of the congregation have been hurt in the past or taken advantage of, and they refuse to get involved.

Passive attitudes arise when there is a lack of vision. Vision brings excitement, commitment, and involvement. Whenever these attitudes are missing, church leaders know something is wrong.

Consolidated power.

One of the outcomes of church fights and splits is the consolidation of power by lay leaders. The loss of close friends brings pain that no one wants to relive. In an effort to protect themselves from additional pain, lay leaders grab the power and keep decision making close to home. Anyone seeking to challenge a lay leader's newfound control is met with strong resistance. What is perceived to threaten the calm is fiercely challenged. If the pastor is perceived to be a part of the problem, people lose respect for the pastoral office and consolidate power and control over all church functions. Directly or indirectly the office is viewed with skepticism. Even a new pastor will face resistance for months, and even years, due to this loss of respect.

Lack of vision.

It is easy for a church to lose vision. While loss of vision is not a volatile issue, over time it saps the energy of a church's ministry. I've found that pastors initially enter into ministry work with hope for the future of the church. Their hope, or vision, is big enough to carry them for at most ten to twelve years, after which the vision is either accomplished or begins to wind down. Numerous pastors have confided that the first ten years in their church were exciting, the next ten tolerable, and the last ten deplorable (most feel they should have left after the twentieth year).

The underlying issue is a loss of vision. Understanding a church's purpose (or mission) provides a biblical reason for church ministry, but it is vision that provides the energy, hope, and passion. When a church and its leaders lose a sense of vision, the ministry starts winding down. As Jon M. Van Dine, an experienced turnaround pastor, notes, "Growth without a shared vision is rare."[2]

Toleration of known sin.

Occasionally, it is unclear why a church is struggling. On the surface everything may look fine. The location might be extremely favorable—accessible, visible, expandable—but the church does not reach its potential. Mission, vision, and goals are in place, but nothing works. Prayer abounds and new ministries are started, all to no avail. In such cases, it is wise to look below the surface, or as church consultant Dan Reeves likes to say, behind the curtain.[3]

If you've ever been to a play, you know that a large curtain on the stage separates the audience from the actors scurrying around in preparation for the performance. In a similar way, ministry has at least two dimensions: public and private. Sunday services, weekly small groups, and other programs are operated in the public domain—that is, in front of the curtain. Personal actions, attitudes, and emotions, what is usually referred to as character, are behind the curtain. When everything looks right in front of the curtain but the church is not producing the expected fruit, it is wise to look behind the curtain at character issues.

After accepting what appeared at first glance to be a fine ministry, a former student of mine soon discovered that open sin on the church board was being ignored. The chairman of the board was involved in a sexual relationship with another member of the church (not his wife). The previous pastor and current board members had refused to confront him about his sin. Upon discovery of this situation, the new pastor brought it to the attention of the board only to discover that other board members were also involved in illicit relationships.

After the new pastor and other board members confronted those in the church involved in the sinful activities, several board members resigned, and some members left the church. It was a difficult first few months, but the courage to confront sin allowed a fresh wind of the Holy Spirit into the life of the church. Growth began nearly overnight as people gained respect for the pastor, board members, and their vision for the future.

Unproductive ministries.

Throughout history, God has blessed certain ministries to reach people for Christ. Nearly every church can point to a time and particular ministry that worked well in the past. It might be a children's program, an approach to evangelism, or even a beloved pastor's unique style of preaching. Sometimes these shadows from the past divert churches from seeing what God wants to do today. It's true that God worked in the past, but he is alive and wants to work today also. An example of this is a church I consulted with a few years ago. It had a large two-story educational wing for children with enough classrooms to comfortably house over three hundred children at one time. Yet on the weekend of my visit to the church, there were less than fifty children in the building. I later discovered that for a number of years the church hosted a popular children's radio program that attracted numerous families. When the pastor—the speaker on the radio program—retired, the program was canceled. Slowly families left the church over the ensuing years. Assessing the situation, I felt there was still great opportunity to reach families and children in the immediate neighborhood. However, as I interviewed church leaders, they kept insisting that the only way to revive the church was to restart the children's radio program. Other churches in the same community were successfully reaching children with basketball programs, soccer camps, and tutoring, but the highly successful children's ministry of years past was casting a shadow that kept leaders from seeing new ways to reach children.

Remove the Fog

Without a doubt, the first thing that must happen before a church can begin a process of revitalization is an admission that there is a problem. Church leaders often fail to see or admit the church's true condition. A fog surrounds their thinking that keeps them from seeing the true state of the church. The fog is removed when leaders assess the situation and determine how quickly to act.

In some situations, it is crucial that action be taken quickly. When a church is in great danger of collapse, there is no time to form a committee to discuss the issue. Something must be done to correct the problem or it will be too late. Churches in slow decline, with a bank of resources, may not be in as desperate a situation. In less-critical situations, church leaders may be able to take time to build a consensus for change.

Revitalization is not always the same as reconstruction. Pastor Ron Tovmassian points out, "When you revitalize a building, you start with what you have, make some changes, tear down some walls and renovate the existing structure into something new and attractive. Much of what was originally there remains and is enhanced by the work that is done. Reconstruction, in contrast, starts with the demolition of the entire existing structure and ends with the construction of a new building where the old one once stood."[4] In a desperate church, it may be necessary to do some reconstruction, while in a stable church, it is more likely that a process of revitalization can take place with good results.

47

A Desperate Church: Move Fast

A desperate church is one that is in danger of closing. Much like a person with a major illness, something must be done immediately if the church is to survive, let alone flourish.

In assessing the situation of your church, consider the following key indicators of a desperate church.

Public worship attendance of fifty people or fewer. It once was assumed that twelve families tithing their income to a church was sufficient to support a full-time pastor with enough money left over to run a basic ministry. It is doubtful whether this was ever factual, but it clearly takes more resources today. At the minimum, it takes double that number, say, twenty-four family units, to provide the needed resources for a traditional church ministry. Many house churches do exist with fewer people and resources, but for a church desiring to offer the basic services of worship, children's ministry, and some adult programming, two dozen family units (assuming at least two people per family unit) are a bare minimum for a church to thrive. If a church drops below that level of worship attendance, it is a sign of looming disaster.

Twenty-five or fewer giving units. A worship attendance of at least fifty people naturally leads to the conclusion that a church also needs at least twenty-five giving units. Take for example a community where the average family income is $50,000. A tithe to a church would equal $5,000, and twenty-five families might contribute $125,000 per year to a church. In such a scenario, there would be sufficient financial resources to pay a pastor's salary and benefits with enough left over to run a basic church ministry program. Unfortunately, the average giving per unit in the United States is in the range of 4 percent rather than 10 percent. Thus, twenty-five giving units in our fictitious community would be giving only $50,000, which would barely allow a pastor to live at the same level of average income as others in the community with no money left over for ministry. Thus, twenty-five giving units is an absolute minimum for a church to survive, unless there are other sources of financial income unrelated to the giving of worshipers.

Less than one leader for every ten people. The Old Testament story of Moses and his father-in-law, Jethro, is a solid standard to use in determining how many leaders a church needs to remain healthy (see Exod. 18). As you will recall, Moses was overworked to the point that the people were frustrated with his lack of availability. Moses was trying to do everything and didn't have time to care for all the mounting needs of the people. Watching from the sidelines, Moses's father-in-law, Jethro, soon offered some suggestions (as fathers-in-law are prone to do). Jethro's advice was to appoint leaders of tens, fifties, hundreds, and thousands. Moses listened to Jethro (a minor miracle in itself), and the problem was solved.

Jethro's advice is a good formula to use in determining the number of leaders needed in a church. For instance, a church of 150 people needs fifteen leaders of ten, three leaders of fifty, and one leader of hundreds. This would likely take shape as ten leaders of small groups or classes, three board members, and one pastor. A church with less than one leader per ten people is likely in trouble. There are not enough leaders to take the church to a new level of ministry.

Average membership tenure of ten years or more. It is good when people remain in a church for a long period of time. A long membership usually signals a high level of commitment and support of the church's ministry. Yet, it is also good when new people are added to a church on a regular basis, as they bring fresh ideas and new resources to bear on the ministry. When newcomers are not incorporated into the life and ministry of a church, it is common for stagnation to abound. Without new blood, a church loses creativity and the ability to attract new people. A sure sign that a church is stagnate (or at least on the road to stagnation) is when the average membership tenure of everyone in the church is greater than ten years. An average of ten years or more points to the fact that not enough new people are being added to the church.

Closely related to average membership tenure is the average age of worshipers as compared to the average age of people in the community. When the average age of people in a church is ten years or more above that of the average age in the community, the church finds it is no longer able to relate to the community. Few visitors walk through the doors of the church, and even fewer come back a second time.

Little identification with the community. In the past, when most churches were started, they related to a specific ethnic majority. Historically, Lutheran churches were started among German peoples, and Reformed churches were started where Dutch families lived. Quite often Baptist churches were planted in African-American communities, and Presbyterian churches were found in Korean neighborhoods. Naturally the music, programs, and organizational structures of such churches reflected the culture of the communities in which they were planted. The evangelism approaches communicated in the idioms of the people found in the community, often with great success.

Over many years, communities change as people move out of the area and new families move in. The open immigration policies found in the United States have even encouraged the movement of people groups from one neighborhood to another. Sometimes a church discovers that its community has changed to the point that the old programs, music, and evangelistic approaches no longer communicate to the groups that now surround the church. If a church does not match the community close enough, it may be a sign of trouble.

CASE STUDY 2
A Desperate Church

Immanuel Baptist Church was founded in a growing suburb of Los Angeles in 1954. The expository Bible teaching of the pastor resonated with the mostly white, middle-class people who moved into the community seeking employment at the local airplane factory and in the hotels, restaurants, and amusement parks being established nearby. Worship attendance peaked at over four hundred in the early 1980s. Since the church was financially strong and a lot was going on, no one gave much notice to the slow decline until worship attendance dropped below one hundred in 1990. Concerned leaders and members of the congregation established a committee to study the reason for the decline, but by 1995 worship attendance stood at seventy-six. From that point things got even worse, as downward momentum set in and worship attendance plummeted to just thirty-four people by 2005.

An analysis of the church revealed that it had been in steady decline for twenty-five years. The average age of church members was fifty, while the average age of people in the surrounding community was just thirty-four. A chart was prepared to show the breakdown of age groups in the community and the church.

Ages	Immanuel Baptist Church	Community
less than 12 yrs	0%	18.8%
12 yrs to 20 yrs	6.45%	10.9%
21 yrs to 34 yrs	3.22%	19.6%
35 yrs to 50 yrs	29.00%	24.1%
over 50 yrs	61.29%	26.6%

Further study revealed that the average worshiper had attended Immanuel Baptist Church for twelve years. Forty-five percent of the people had attended the church for over twelve years, but only 10 percent of the congregation had been attending less than two years.

Most shocking was the change in ethnic diversity during the history of the church. Latinos and Asians now dominated what had started out as a mostly white community. The church no longer matched the people in the community, and church ministries did not speak to the felt needs of the new people. A chart showed the ethnic breakdown in the church compared to that of the community.

51

Ethnicity	Immanuel Baptist Church	Community
Black	0%	2.5%
Latino	9%	39.7%
Asian	13%	26.7%
Caucasian	78%	31.1%

Additional findings pointed to internal issues that were weighing the church down. For example, pastoral tenure over the fifty-six-year history of the church was just 3.5 years per pastor. The facility was over fifty years old, and the attendance of only thirty-four people made for an extremely uncomfortable feeling in the 250-seat sanctuary.

Insights: Immanuel Baptist Church is clearly a desperate church, as indicated by the following signs:

- over two decades of decline
- fewer than twenty-five giving units
- average membership tenure of twelve years
- a mismatch between the average age of church members (fifty years old) and the average age of people in the community (thirty-four years old)
- a mismatch between the ethnic makeup of the church (78% white) and the ethnic makeup of the community (67% Latino and Asian)

A Stable Church: Move Fast, Slowly

Some churches remain the same size for years: up a little, down a little, but always able to hold their own. Being on a plateau is often a comfortable place, with little to threaten the life of the congregation. A plateau is much like hypertension, which is called the silent killer by medical professionals. Hypertension has few, if any, outward symptoms, but its effects over a long period of time are still life-threatening. A church on a long-term plateau faces a similar situation. Plateaus, at least ones that last for three or more years, are life-threatening, silent killers. This is particularly true when the plateau has lasted one or two decades.

Plateaued churches come in all sizes, but straight-line attendance at any size usually signals the need for revitalization. For example, the church illustrated in figure 4 has a decadal growth rate of +4.9 percent. The church is not in a desperate situation, but nonetheless it is not making much headway and may be entirely stagnant. Further research would be needed to determine the exact situation, but a graph like this should alert church leaders that something is keeping the church on a plateau.

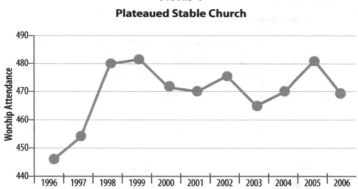

FIGURE 4
Plateaued Stable Church

A growth rate that is less than 25 percent a decade, or 2.3 percent a year, is life-threatening for almost all churches. True, as some have noted, in communities with rapid population turnover, just staying even is a victory. However, such contexts are rarely found outside of towns with a large military, university, or corporate business presence. Determining a church's decadal growth rate is one measurement of health and ought to be taken as seriously as high blood pressure in people. It may take years, but serious damage occurs unless high blood pressure is lowered. Likewise, serious damage is done in a church if a long-term plateau is not corrected.

In a stable church, pastoral leadership is normally granted by the congregation after effective ministry. The process is a continual and constant exchange between the leader and the congregation. Thus, you have time to lead the church in a self-assessment and planning process. *You* do not assess them; rather, *they* assess themselves. At the least, a church should assess its growth/decline, ministry priorities (budget expenditures), involvement priorities (people expenditure), and scriptural priorities (Great Commission). See case study 3 for an illustration of how one church successfully assessed and planned for the future.[5]

CASE STUDY 3
A Stable Church

Pastor Clay accepted a call to Trinity Temple Church knowing that the church was plateaued. The plateau in growth went back nearly twenty years, but the real issue Pastor Clay encountered was a lack of passion for outreach and evangelism. Church members were coasting along year after year without much concern for anything except keeping the doors of the church open for their own use.

Knowing that Trinity was not in any immediate danger of collapse, Pastor Clay called the board and other leaders together for a weekend planning retreat. The first evening he asked everyone to sit at three tables. Then he gave one group an unopened box of children's crayons, he handed a few pens with different colored inks to those at the second table, and to the last team he gave felt-tipped pens of various colors. He then distributed tablets of graph paper and a sheet listing the average yearly statistics of worship attendance, Sunday school attendance, and church membership for the last decade. He explained that each table was to make a graph of one of the areas and then discuss what they saw in the graph. Each group was to come up with questions inspired by what they saw as well as possible explanations for what they found.

After allowing thirty minutes for each group to draw, discuss, and come up with a list of questions, Pastor Clay had one person from each group stand up, show their graph to the rest of the leaders, and explain it. Each group was surprised at what they discovered, and several excellent questions were raised and discussed during the remainder of the evening. On Saturday, the leaders developed a mission statement and a vision statement and set two-year goals. It took all day to arrive at an agreed-upon plan of action, but by Saturday evening, a workable plan for the next two years was in place.

Pastor Clay later commented, "It was a lengthy process, but the end result is we have grown. We are not setting any records, and no one is going to write a book about our church, but when you consider we had been on a plateau for over twenty years, it has been remarkable. Through this planning process, we found three keys to growth. The first is admitting there is a problem. Our evaluation of the last decade helped us see our stagnant situation. The second is repenting. True repentance means turning around and going in a new direction. Once we admitted our lack of passion, we took time to pray and repent, asking God to forgive our lackadaisical attitude. The third key is being intentional. We renewed our mission statement, came up with a fresh vision, and then set some goals that could be accomplished in two years. At the end of two years, we are going to meet again for another planning retreat, redraw our graphs, and make a new plan for the next two years."

Pastor Clay had already drawn the graphs of worship attendance, Sunday school attendance, and membership and knew what the leaders would see. However, instead of telling the church leaders what he had found, he helped them discover it for themselves. He also seeded the planning sessions with Bible verses and ideas he had previously thought about, but he resisted coming to the meeting with a completed plan. Instead, he led the leaders to develop their own plan, using some of his insights and ideas used throughout the sessions.

When it was all over, the leaders owned the plan because it was theirs, not just the pastor's.

Insights:

- Pastor Clay did his own study to determine if the church was desperate or stable.
- Knowing he had time, he designed a plan to help his leaders gain ownership of the revitalization process.
- Instead of telling his leaders what he had already discovered, he helped them discover it for themselves.

Use an Outside Consultant and/or Coach

Have you ever watched someone playing checkers, chess, or some other similar type of game? If so, you may have observed that you can read the game better than those playing it, even though you may not be as good of a player. Why is it that observers watching a game have the ability to read the game better than those playing it? When people play checkers, their own moves trap them. They become so caught up in thinking about the moves they are going to make that they do not see their opponent's moves or the entire flow of the game itself. People who are watching a game are not trapped by their own moves. They are able to remain detached enough to see the game from both players' perspectives. This is one of the major differences between professional and amateur players: amateurs see the game from their perspective; professionals see the game from their opponent's perspective.

Eighty-five percent of pastors looked to outside resources to help initiate or stimulate the turnaround.

JOHN C. LaRue Jr.

Sometimes pastors and other church leaders cannot see the problems and opportunities in their own church. They are so engaged in the action that they find it difficult to see the entire picture. As church leaders and pastors become involved in their own interests, options are overlooked that may be obvious to a more objective person. We've all heard the statement, "You can't see the forest for the trees." A consultant has no axe to grind, no hurt feelings or hidden agendas to cloud the issues. Outside consultants also have a broader range of experiences and a greater exposure to ideas and resources than the normal church member. They bring with them a wide knowledge of proven processes that may be applied to a church to help it reach its overall growth potential. Using the services of an outside consultant or coach is a positive way to assist a church in its efforts toward revitalization.[6]

Bringing It Home

1. Which of the signs of trouble do you see in your church? What other indications are there that revitalization is a growing need?

2. Is your church a stable or a desperate church? How do you know?

3. How quickly do you need to act? What specific insights do you see pointing in that direction?

4. Do you think you can lead the church in the effort of revitalization, or would the use of an outside consultant or coach be of help? What makes you feel this way?

Learn the Principles

Revitalization is a spiritual process.

TERRY WALLING

Churches are different. Smaller churches face challenges different from those of larger ones. Midsized churches struggle with issues that smaller churches never encounter. Rural churches must make decisions that urban churches do not need to make. That said, there are essential principles of revitalization that work in all churches.

Revitalization Is a Spiritual Issue

At its root, revitalization is a spiritual issue. In a study reported in *Your Church*, the number one change made in churches that turned around was spiritual, such as added prayer initiatives.

Seventy-five percent of the revitalized churches reported starting such initiatives.[1] Pastors and other church leaders regularly overlook this key point, preferring to focus on organizational or facility or program issues. This is not surprising, since dealing with spiritual issues, such as confrontation of known sin, is a challenging part of ministry. It is a mistake, however, to ignore the spiritual dynamic of revitalization.

As you begin the process of revitalizing a church, establish high morals, ethics, and credibility and stick to them. Show your people daily that these principles are more than words—that they live and thrive in you. Leaders who lack such principles are doomed to fail. Consider the following principles of revitalization and begin using them today.

Revitalization happens when known sin is confessed.

Biblical writers speak of the concept of repentance rather than turnaround. In the Old Testament, the Hebrew word for repentance (*shuv*) means to turn or return. This word is used in the following well-known passage: "[If] My people who are called by My name humble themselves and pray and seek My face and turn [*shuv*] from their wicked ways, then I will hear from heaven, will forgive their sin and will heal their land" (2 Chron. 7:14). For the people of Israel to be revitalized, they had to not only seek God but also turn from their wicked ways and go in a new direction. I like the comment Hebrew scholar Walter C. Kaiser makes: "The Hebrew word 'to turn or repent' is pronounced *shuv*. And in every one of the 118 instances where the word occurs with a religious significance, God was trying to give his people a *shove* in the right direction."[2]

Most churches I've worked with are willing to seek God in prayer, asking him to renew their church. What they are not willing to do is turn from their wicked ways. Based on my experience, few churches need to repent from sexual or ethical sins (although some do). Most need to repent from a lack of love for the lost, a loss of passion for God's mission, and

60

bitterness toward their fellow Christians. It is quite common to find older churches that harbor deep anger and hurt resulting from past disruptions, such as church splits, which have never been forgiven. Revitalization begins with prayers of contrition and confession and also acts of restitution for ills perpetrated in the past. Revitalization begins when church members admit they have a problem. As you begin the revitalization process, lead your church in contrition and confession. If acts of injustice have been committed against former members or pastors, make things right.[3]

> *Maybe this is where real turnarounds have to start: with leaders and people bowed low, in silence, listening to Jesus.*
> GORDON MACDONALD

Revitalization happens by focusing on the possibilities.

Revitalization leaders understand the problems, but they focus on the possibilities. Doing the opposite—focusing on the problems—is demoralizing to yourself and to your people. Revitalization is an inside job. It starts in your own heart and head. Positive leaders keep looking to the next action steps they need to take rather than worrying about what took place in the past. Worrying never solves a problem; planning does. Problems are distractions that pull your energy away from your dreams and plans, so ask, What is one thing I can do today that will move me, and the church, in a positive direction? Be proactive in the pursuit of your goals. Think of it this way. If you did one thing, no matter how small, each day to further your goal of revitalization, in one year you would have performed 365 positive actions. That many positive actions are bound to make a positive impact. Do this for five years and you will have completed 1,825 positive actions!

I suggest you set up a daily revitalization journal and record all the positive actions you perform throughout each day to move the church forward. If you encourage a board member, write it down as a positive accomplishment. Did you pray for God's direction? Write it down as a positive action. Was a new visitor present at church on Sunday? Record it in your journal. Did the congregation clean up the church property last Saturday? Put it down. Record anything and everything that is positive.

Every night before you go to bed, write down as many positive actions for that day as possible. If you can't think of anything positive, write, "God is with me in this project." He is, right? And that's positive. So write it down. Then before you go to sleep, glance through your journal and thank God for the positives you read. Do this at night right before you go to bed. Why? Research has found that what we think about before we go to sleep stays in our subconscious minds throughout our sleep. Have you ever watched a scary movie at night and then found it difficult to sleep? Did you ever have an argument with someone close to bedtime and then tossed and turned all night? What we think about right before bedtime stays with us. So read your journal. Doing so will have a powerful impact on your beliefs and actions.

Revitalization happens through small victories celebrated along the way.

The people in churches needing a turnaround are usually discouraged. Years of struggle, perhaps even a church split or two, may have created feelings of hopelessness. They are not ready for a big vision or challenge. You will need to create a series of small successes—baby steps—to build up their faith. Short-term projects, such as painting the auditorium, replacing carpet in classrooms, or restoring the landscape around the facilities, can help build up faith.

Make a list of several small projects that can be done quickly. Completing them will give you some early wins and assist in raising the morale of the congregation. Members will realize they can do something positive. These early wins will also increase their trust in your leadership. One warning: be cautious not to tackle too large of a project. You need to build confidence in small steps. Each project should be a bit larger or more challenging than the last, but in the beginning, make sure you can complete it.

Revitalization happens as ministry emphasis shifts from members to people in the community.

My friend Ken Priddy says, "You evangelize to revitalize; you don't revitalize to evangelize." I agree. Most churches I've observed believe they must get better inwardly before they can reach out to those in the community. If, as mentioned previously, a church has known sin that needs confessing, this is true. No one wants to bring new believers into a church where sin is clearly present and not confronted. However, many church leaders feel that if they focus on the spiritual formation of the congregation, people will naturally reach out in evangelism. I have not observed this to be a fact of life in churches. In my experience, when churches focus inwardly, they never focus outwardly. They never reach a point where they sense they are healthy enough to evangelize and therefore never do.

> *You evangelize to revitalize; you don't revitalize to evangelize.*
> KEN PRIDDY

On the other hand, when leaders shift the focus from those already in the church to those in the community, the church is revitalized and the people in the church experience spiritual growth. Consider how Jesus trained his disciples. Did he wait until they were spiritually mature before he sent them out in ministry to the community? Of course not. He sent them out *before* they were mature. In the process, they encountered questions they couldn't answer, problems they couldn't solve, and people they couldn't handle. The result? They came back to Jesus ready to listen, learn, and grow. Spiritual maturity flows out of ministry.

Get the church involved in outreach and evangelism as steps toward revitalization. Consider that outreach and evangelism are two different things. Outreach is service-oriented, or what today is frequently called missional service. Serving our communities through social action projects, working in partnership with local public schools, and a host of other activities are ways of reaching out to the community. By so doing, a church establishes a caring presence in the community and builds trust among those it hopes to reach. Evangelism is conversion-oriented. While churches certainly are right to serve others, they are called to do more. Churches are called to make disciples by preaching the Good News of salvation through the death and resurrection of Jesus Christ. This means that, ultimately, churches must find ways to proclaim the gospel of salvation to those they serve as well as challenge them to convert to belief in Jesus Christ. Revitalization really takes hold as people already in a church begin to reach out in outreach and evangelism to those in their community.

Revitalization happens as deeply ingrained patterns of dysfunctional behavior are diagnosed, admitted, and cured.

A friend of mine accepted an appointment to a church not long ago. The second week he was there, the board chairperson took him to breakfast and told him that he wanted the pastor to get his approval on all sermon topics before he preached. The chairperson said, "I've always been in charge, and everything will go well if that is understood." This misuse of power had led to an average pastoral tenure in the church of only two years as pastors fled from this dysfunctional leader. It was a systemic power and control issue that had to be dealt with before the church could be revitalized.

Another pastor told me that his church had four boards that were all equal. They could never agree on the mission or vision of the future because one board would always veto what another board desired to do. This organizational structure had worked well for many years under the leadership of a strong senior pastor who knew how to work the system. But when that powerful pastor retired, the structure became an issue that stalled the church for over two decades. It was only after the four-board system was changed to a single board that ministry began to turn around.

Case Study 4
Using Principles of Revitalization

Rev. George recognized immediately that his new church was in trouble. The former pastor had served well for eight years but had not provided any direction for the church. With his focus on spiritual formation, the previous pastor had left a church that was loving, caring, and without conflict, but attendance had declined every year of his eight-year tenure. Everyone in the church knew something had to be done to stop the decline or the church would be in danger of closing.

During his first month at the church, Rev. George spent a lot of time listening to other people. It was during one of these listening sessions over lunch that one leader's comment caught him by surprise. Pastor George had asked the leaders, "What do you think we need to do?" One leader replied, "I don't know, but it won't get done unless you do it." At that point, Rev. George knew he should just take charge. The situation was dire, and the people were handing him the baton and saying, "Give us direction."

The next week he called the board together. Together they charted a one-year plan that included holiday celebrations (Thanksgiving, Christmas, Easter) and all church events (vacation Bible school, Christmas carol sing, Good Friday observance). This simple procedure gave the leaders confidence that the church was moving forward.

Later, Rev. George encouraged church members to do some needed refurbishing around the church. Nothing big at first, just simple things like painting the church sign, clearing brush from the churchyard, and sprucing up the lobby. None of this took much money. People enjoyed working together, and their morale rose a bit.

The major adventure agreed upon by everyone was to host a trunk 'n' treat on Halloween night at the church. Again, this didn't take much work or expense. Each church family purchased candy to give away, drove to the church parking lot on Halloween night, decorated the trunks of their cars, and handed out candy to the neighborhood children. The church advertised the event at the local elementary school and at neighborhood stores. The week of Halloween a team of people distributed pamphlets in the immediate vicinity of the church. It was the first outreach event held by the church in nearly a decade, and everyone agreed to do it again the next year.

The major challenge Rev. George faced was the presence of a negative board member. The board member owned a home in Florida and was often away five to six months a year. Of course, decisions had to be made while he was gone, but then he always became angry when he returned, which caused much stress among other board members. Fortunately, at one board meeting, the angry board member offered to resign, and Rev. George immediately accepted his resignation, which shocked everyone present. Evidently the angry board member had offered to resign many times in the past, but Rev. George was the first one to call his bluff by accepting his resignation.

At the end of the year, the church had gained fifteen worshipers, rising from an average of sixty-five to eighty. Morale was high, as church members saw hope for the future.

Analysis:

- What led to the increased morale among church members?

- How did the church begin to focus on people outside the church?
- What systemic power and control issues surfaced, and how were they handled?
- What would Rev. George want to do in your church to get it started on the road to revitalization?

Questions to Consider

To revitalize a church, you cannot do ministry as usual. You have to work as if you were starting from scratch. There is no safety in playing it safe. Before you begin, however, it is wise to look in the mirror and ask yourself some tough questions about your church and yourself. So take the time right now to consider the following questions before you stir up church leaders and members of the congregation with dreams of a new day of ministry.

What is your purpose?

Review the purpose of your church. What are you trying to accomplish through your ministry? If your church lacks an up-to-date statement of its purpose, work with key leaders to develop a new one. Your purpose statement should be less than twenty-five words in length so that it can be communicated easily. Take the time to communicate your purpose to the entire church, as it gives you the biblical reason for developing a new model of ministry.

Is your present model of ministry accomplishing your purpose?

Ask your leaders to compare the purpose statement with what they are doing. Put together several working teams (not committees) and ask them to evaluate your church in light of your purpose statement. Honestly evaluate the extent to which you are fulfilling your God-given purpose. If you find that your present model of ministry accomplishes your purpose, there may be no need to begin another model of ministry. Obviously, if your purpose is not being reached, you should consider selecting a new model of ministry that will be more effective.

Whom are you trying to reach?

Begin by determining who you are as a church. While the current makeup of your congregation should not be an excuse for failure to reach out to those unlike you, it does limit to some extent those you can reach effectively. Once you know who you are, develop a population profile of the people in your ministry area. Obtain demographic information showing the percentages of different groups of people in your area.

Are there people who will support this cause?

Orchestrating a new model of ministry takes the combined energy and faith of many people. Do not take on the burden of such a process alone. Look over the available leadership. Is there a core group of people who are willing to pay the price to see the new model of ministry take shape? If none can be found, begin to share your vision for a new model of ministry with key people, asking God to build a team of committed leaders.

Have you been at the church long enough?

As a rule, a pastoral tenure of more than four years is the minimum needed to bring about significant change. The only major exception to this rule occurs when a church is in a desperate situation. Stable churches give their full allegiance to church leaders only after the leadership has instilled confidence in the congregation through credible ministry. Do the people of the church trust the leaders? Have you been at the church long enough to establish respect?

Are you willing to finish the job?

Research in the field of church growth shows that it takes an average of seven years to implement significant changes in an urban or suburban church. Bringing about the same changes in a rural setting often takes ten to twelve years, if not longer. If the new model of ministry is implemented, will you, other church leaders, and staff remain at the church long enough to see it through to completion? It is unethical to lead a congregation to adopt a new form of ministry and then abandon it.

Is your church worth changing?

Take a long look at the location of your church. Is it in the right location? If you were planting your church today, would you select its present site? If not, experience suggests it is wise not to put your people through the pain of change unless it will assist them in getting to the proper location. For example, an established church in a poor location would do best to start a satellite church in a more desirable location. This strategy allows a church to establish a point of ministry in a place where it should eventually be relocated.

Is your church flexible enough to face the future?

The difference between an older and a younger church is related to two aspects of life: controllability and flexibility. Younger churches have less controls in the sense of having fewer rules and regulations. Older churches typically have numerous policies and guidelines that create controls (some unnecessary) that serve to keep the church stable. Younger churches have lower controllability, and older ones have greater controllability. While it is necessary to do things decently and in order (controllability), too many controls result in a church that is inflexible. Fewer rules and regulations allow younger churches to try new ministries, stop investing in programs that don't work, and move in new directions. Older churches, with myriad policies, guidelines, and regulations, may find it difficult to start a new ministry or close an ineffective one. A younger church has few controls and greater flexibility to start new programs. An older church has many controls and less flexibility when it comes to starting something new. Is your church old or young? Flexible or inflexible? The more flexible it is, the easier it will be to revitalize.

Is the time right?

The Bible is full of agricultural imagery, and if there is one thing we learn from agriculture, it is the importance of timing. As anyone who has worked on a farm or a ranch or just planted a backyard garden realizes, there are distinct times for tilling, planting, watering, weeding, fertilizing, and harvesting. Paul referred to such a cycle when he wrote, "I planted, Apollos watered, but God was causing the growth" (1 Cor. 3:6). I've noticed that God gives some pastors a tilling ministry, while others serve as planters. One pastor may water, and then another pastor may harvest the fruit. My prayer is that every pastor would get the chance to have a harvesting ministry, but the truth is that many serve in the hard work of tilling, planting, watering, weeding, and fertilizing without ever seeing a harvest in the life of a church.

What stage is your church in? Is it the time of harvest? Are you facing a time of tilling the ground, which has hardened over the years, perhaps having to deal with hidden sins in the congregation? Or is it a time of planting seeds of ideas, possibilities, and hope? Depending on the timing, your people may be ready to change. Or they may need lengthy preparation. Where is your church at this moment?

Do you have the money or other resources?

There are monetary costs involved in revitalization, such as those needed to renovate a church building, engage in relocation, or start a new program. There are also social costs, such as the congregation's emotional capacity for change and their willingness to follow your leadership. What are you up against? Is there emotional trust between leaders and the congregation? What must be done to build the financial and emotional resources?

Is the church at risk?

Churches come in different sizes and are located in different contexts. Churches of one hundred or five hundred or one thousand people that stay at the same size year after year may not feel the same level of danger. Depending on their contextual situation, they may be at great risk of closing the doors forever or just at a slight risk of a loss of energy. As noted in the last chapter, the greater the risk (a desperate church), the faster you must work and the more directive you must be in your leadership style. The lower the risk (a stable church), the more time you have to build relationships, consensus, and vision.

Why do you want to revitalize the church?

This may be the most important question. Is your motive to show people you can do it? Do you fear being seen as a failure? Is it important to raise your self-esteem? The answer should be that you want to be more fruitful in making disciples. Ask yourself a simple question: Is this decision consistent with making disciples for Jesus Christ? If the answer is yes, you are doing the right thing.

Bringing It Home

1. Are there obvious or hidden spiritual issues standing in the way of revitalizing your church? If so, how do you plan to address them?

2. Are there deeply ingrained dysfunctional habits or practices that need to be diagnosed, admitted, and cured? If so, how do you plan on speaking to such issues?

3. Is your church focused primarily on the spiritual formation of present worshipers, or are you reaching out to those who need Christ but are not yet in your church?

4. In the section "Questions to Consider," which were the most thought provoking? Why?

5

Discern God's Vision

**Church
Revitalization
Chart**

See the Potential

Commit to Lead

Assess the Situation

Learn the Principles

Discern God's Vision

Build a Coalition

Lift the Morale

Make Hard Decisions

Refocus the Ministry

Equip for Change

Deal with Resistance

Stay the Course

Breaking Through

*We must get a vision of God before we can get
a vision from God.*

KEN PRIDDY

A few years ago my wife and I decided to take a cruise to Alaska. Even though we live in Southern California, we grew up in Colorado and prefer a little cooler climate. Going to the cold climate of Alaska appealed to us. We'd always seen pictures of Alaska, and the thought of seeing one of the huge glaciers found there was also exciting. When we put a date on the calendar (at the time five years away) and started saving money for the trip, our hopes grew. The Alaskan trip became a vision for which we dreamed, worked, and planned.

To revitalize a church, you need to know two things: where the church is and where you want it to go. Once you've evaluated your situation and determined that the church is worth saving, you must then decide where it should go. A vision is simply a description of hope for the future. It is a description of what you desire to accomplish. To be even more direct, a vision is not what *you* want but rather what *God* wants for your church.

What Is Vision, Really?

One way to understand vision is to see it as the intersection of the pastor's leadership passion, the passion and gifts of the congregation, and the community needs (see fig. 5). Where these three concepts intersect is the vision God has for your church. For example, if the pastor has a passion for education, and the congregation has members with gifts of teaching, and the community has a need for better schools, God's vision may be for your church to start a Christian school. However, if the pastor is not passionate about education, or you don't have teachers in your church, this may not be a wise direction in which to head.

> *In evaluating churches that are growing and healthy as well as those that are stagnant or in decline, one of the key distinctions that emerges between these categories is the existence of true vision for ministry.*
>
> GEORGE BARNA

At this stage, you don't need to know all the steps it will take to get where God wants you to go. The important point is to determine in which direction to head. God will give you the necessary information when you need it. In fact, God works with you somewhat like a GPS. A Global Positioning System just needs to know where you are and where you want to go. After you type in these two coordinates, the technology works with three satellites and, as you travel along the road, gives you directions. If you use a GPS in your car, you understand what this technology does.

74

FIGURE 5

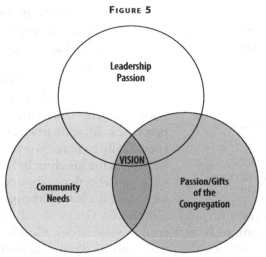

Reprinted by permission from Tom Harper and the Society for Church Consulting.

God works in a similar manner in guiding you. Once you know where you are as a church and start moving in the direction you want to go, he gives you directions to get there. As you clarify your vision and focus in on it with your plans and goals, God will lead you. But just like a GPS in your car, the directions always come just before you need them.

So how do you discover God's vision for your church? Here's a practical approach I've found workable in several churches. It's just a plan, so feel free to adjust it as you need so it fits your particular church and context.

How to Discern God's Vision

Engage in personal Bible reading and prayer.

Vision starts with the pastor. Take a moment and glance through the Bible and notice to whom God gives vision. You'll find that God gives vision to a single person rather than a group of people. Rarely does God give vision to a committee, a board, or a team of people. These groups are important, but they typically serve to help a leader shape and form a vision rather than discover it. So if you are a pastor, vision begins with you.

Start by reading the Bible, asking God to show you what he wants for your church. Contemplate God's priorities. In your prayers, ask God specifically to make you alert to what he desires for his church. Keep a journal or notebook nearby and jot down any and all ideas that pop into your mind as you pray and meditate on God's Word. Allow your own passion to be reflected in your notes. God has put you in this church for this time, and he likely has been shaping his vision in you long before you arrived. Be sure to confess any known sin in your own life as well as any you observe in the church's past or present.

> *The future belongs to those who believe in the beauty of their dreams.*
>
> ELEANOR ROOSEVELT

Two passages of Scripture are good to reflect on at this point. The first is Isaiah 6:1–8. Notice that Isaiah first sees God, then sees himself, only after which does God give Isaiah a vision for his work. After Isaiah saw God, he was highly aware of his own sinfulness, which led to his confession of being a man of unclean lips. This is where vision begins: with confession.

The second passage is Nehemiah 1:1–11. As he prayed for the future revitalization of Israel, Nehemiah identified with the sins of the people, even though he may not have been involved in the sin directly. He prayed, "On behalf of the sons of Israel Your servants, confessing the sins of the sons of Israel which *we have sinned* against You" (v. 6, emphasis added). If you are aware of any congregational sins, it is wise to confess them to God as you pray for vision to be revealed.

As part of this process, find two or three people you trust and ask them to be on your prayer team. Sometimes these people are found in the church you serve, but at other times you will need to look outside your local church for team members. Once the team is in place, ask members to pray that God's dream for the future of your church will become clear. Communicate with them on a weekly basis. Email is okay, but remember that emails can and do get passed around, so be cautious about what you put into an email. A personal conversation is best. This prayer team will become a vital link for you as you work to revitalize your church.

It is also good to develop an intercessory prayer team in your church. I suggest you begin looking for what used to be called "prayer warriors." *Intercessor* is the more common term today and generally means a person who prays one hour a day. One way to find intercessors is to ask people in your church, "If you needed someone to pray for you, whom would you ask?" If you hear the same person mentioned over and over, he or she is likely an intercessor. When you can identify a minimum of three intercessors, form them into a prayer team for your church. This is a different prayer team than the pastor's prayer team. This is an intercessory team for the church. Once this team is in place, ask members to focus their prayers on the formation of a vision for the future of the church. Later you can ask the intercessory team to pray about different issues, but start with vision.

Analyze the church and its community.

During the time you are reading God's Word and praying, do some fieldwork concerning the community and the church. Read local newspapers and make notes in your journal about community concerns and struggles. Talk with leaders in your town, such as policemen, politicians, and real estate agents, and listen to their heart regarding the community. Ask neighbors living around your church how they think a church could help out in the community.

Be sure to talk to church members and worshipers. The following five questions are helpful in determining a vision for the future.

1. How does God want to express himself through this church in this community at this time?
2. If our church building burned down, would we rebuild it the same? If not, what would we change?
3. If we were starting our church from scratch, what would we do differently?
4. If we knew our church was going to close in the next year, what would we do today?
5. What is God doing in our community, and how can we get on board?

Remember, God is already at work in your community. What is he blessing? Is it preschools? Then perhaps starting a preschool should be part of your vision. Is it Saturday evening worship services? Then maybe starting a Saturday night worship service should be part of your vision. Is it recovery ministry? Then consider starting a recovery ministry.

Share your vision.

Unless your church is in a desperate situation, allow time to think and let your thoughts ruminate. To ruminate means to chew on something awhile, which is exactly what cows do. It may be an unpleasant picture to some, but cows chew on their food, swallow it, then bring it up again and chew on it some more before swallowing it again. Rumination means to think about something, lay it aside, and then later on think about it some more. Such activity is important when developing a vision. As you read God's Word, pray, and talk to community and church leaders, allow God time to create thoughts and passions in your mind. What you'll discover is that God brings some thoughts to the surface, while other ideas will vanish.

As God develops specific ideas in your heart and mind, begin writing them down into a formal statement of a vision for the future. Try to paint a picture of what you think God desires your church to do. But whatever you do, don't share it openly and don't preach it to the congregation. Instead, take time to talk with leaders one-on-one. Ask them

> *Vision matures over time, sprouting branches of new opportunities.*
>
> KEN PRIDDY

where they think God wants the church to go in the future, and then listen carefully. When they are finished, tell them you've been thinking and praying a lot about this lately. Ask if you can share what you've been thinking. They will, certainly, say it's okay to do so. Then share your thoughts and ask what they think about them. Do this with every leader one-on-one.

Host a vision retreat.

After you've taken the time to share your initial vision ideas with the leaders, call for a vision retreat. It is best to start on a Friday evening and go all day Saturday. Begin on Friday evening with some evaluation, such as that mentioned in the last chapter. Then on Saturday use something like the following schedule:

8:00–8:30	breakfast
8:30–9:00	worship and corporate prayer time (Take time to sing and pray together. Confess any known sin and ask God to reveal his vision for the future to you this day.)
9:00–9:45	private prayer time (Instruct those present to go away by themselves to read the Bible and pray. Give them a short list of Bible verses you want them to reflect on and pray about.)
9:45–10:00	refreshment break

10:00–12:00	discussion of vision (Begin the discussion with your suggested vision statement, which you have revised after talking privately with all the church leaders. Ask what they might add, change, or modify. Work to gain agreement on the direction for the future of your church. The five questions listed on p. 78 are good ones to ask during this session.)
12:00–1:00	lunch
1:00–3:00	planning (Assuming you've reached agreement on the vision, come up with one to two years' worth of goals to help you put the vision into place.)
3:00–3:30	prayers and dismissal

CASE STUDY 5

Vision Development

During Pastor John's morning devotions, he had been drawn to several Bible passages that highlighted the fact that God sent Jesus to earth to minister to humankind, and then Jesus sent his disciples to serve others. He started to reflect on the fact that God had sent his church into its community to serve others too.

It just happened that he had recently met the principal of the local grade school, which was located directly across the street from the church. One day the principal was standing on the street outside the school just as Pastor John arrived, and, having waved at each other for several months, Pastor John decided it was time they met. After introducing himself, Pastor John casually inquired about any possible needs the school might have with which the church might be able to help. At first the principal couldn't think of anything, but then, after some thought, he mentioned that the teachers were short on paper for their classrooms.

As Pastor John thought about the missional nature of Jesus and his church, an idea (some would say a vision) popped into his mind. He wondered if his church could supply the paper the teachers needed. Actually, his thoughts were larger than just supplying paper. Pastor John was envisioning a partnership between his church and the local public school whereby his church would adopt the school and its staff and provide

80

assistance as needed. Would his church accept this as appropriate for a church's vision? More problematic was whether the public school would partner with a church.

Pastor John jotted down some ideas and started talking with his leaders. One by one they started to see the potential of the partnership and agreed it might be possible. With his leaders' approval, Pastor John made an appointment with the principal to discuss his idea. It took several meetings, but eventually the principal and staff gave approval to test the partnership. Pastor John rallied the people at church, funds were raised, and the paper was purchased and delivered. At the end of the school year, Pastor John's church provided a thank-you luncheon for the teachers and presented each teacher with a small appreciation gift.

This happened five years ago, and the partnership has flourished. The church has carefully provided love and care for the teachers, staff, and principal without any religious overtones or obligations. But some teachers have begun attending the church on their own.

Analysis:

- How did Pastor John discover God's vision for his church?
- How was the vision shared and owned by the leaders?
- How did the vision come to fruition? What process took place that might be illustrative for your own church?

Create the Future from Your Future

As I travel around the United States visiting churches, I've noticed that nearly every one has a communion table on which is written a biblical statement. On the majority of communion tables I've seen the phrase "This Do in Remembrance of Me." This statement points to the past when God, through Jesus Christ, worked his act of redemption. Lately,

I've noticed that more and more communion tables have a different phrase: "until he comes." This statement points in a different direction—to the future. Both the past acts of God and the future acts of God are important. He did act on our behalf in the past. However, that act of redemption was done once and for all. We are called to remember it, but he is not called to relive it. What he did for us in the past is phenomenal, but he is working for us right now even if we sometimes don't see him. The fact that the church is still in existence points to his grace in keeping it alive even if it is not as fruitful as we wish. And he will work for us in the future. The same God who worked mightily for the church in the past still desires to work mightily for us today and in the coming years.

> *Can there be anything worse than losing one's eyesight? Yes, losing your vision.*
>
> ANONYMOUS

While it is right and proper to remember what God has done in your church in the past, you live in the present and hope for the future. A church's vision can't be developed from its past. The vision can't be a return to the past. Vision must be built on future hopes and dreams. Your church's vision should be created from the future, not the past.

Bringing It Home

1. Does your church understand God's vision for its future?

2. How do your Sunday worshipers demonstrate ownership of the vision?

3. If you don't have a clearly articulated vision of the future, what ideas from this chapter might you be able to use?

4. How does your personal passion, the passion and gifts of your congregation, and the needs of your community intersect? How could this intersection be formed into a workable vision for the future?

82

6

Build a Coalition

You've got to get the right people on the bus.

JIM COLLINS

Before becoming a pastor, I worked for a short time as a manager of three electronics stores. It was there that I first learned what it was like to have executive authority. In each store, I had the authority to hire and fire workers. I could tell the employees what to do, and they did it. I set the schedules and the work rules and generally directed the sales force in every detail of the working day. The power of the paycheck gave me executive authority in motivating my employees.

After I transitioned into the role of pastor, I discovered that the power map is quite different. Churches, like other nonprofit organizations, rely on volunteers. Without the power of the paycheck, pastors have to rely on a more relational type of

83

authority to get things done. Writing about leadership in non-profit organizations, Jim Collins says that leaders have to "architect the condition for the right decisions to happen. That's a much more nuanced, much more difficult leadership. And, it's a much more difficult version of power. To be able to figure out how to assemble power to make things happen is real, real leadership."[1]

As a pastor, you may see the danger your church is facing. If you are in a desperate church, you will need to execute whatever degree of executive authority you possess to build a coalition of people to help as quickly as possible. In most churches, especially stable ones, you can gradually assemble a team of people to help you get the job done. The technical term for this team is a *dominant coalition*.

A Dominant Coalition

A coalition is a group of people who come together to accomplish a task. They work together to guide an organization, in this case a church, to accomplish its essential purpose. If your church has been around for some time, a dominant coalition already exists in your church. Some dominant coalitions are representative of the entire congregation (perhaps an elected board), others are collaborative (people who talk together and decide to vote as a group), and some (in smaller churches) are a single family or two. Sometimes this group is referred to as the shareholders or the stakeholders of the church. They may be major donors or perhaps the matriarch and the patriarch of the church. Lyle Schaller labeled them *pioneers*, that is, those leaders who started the church years before and have kept it going in the years since.[2] Who are the past, current, and future leaders of your church? They are likely your current dominant coalition.

> *Forty-two percent of pastors reported that the church board was the number one source of resistance to the turnaround plan.*
>
> JOHN C. LARUE JR.

George's Buckets of Berries Theory

A number of years ago, church consultant Carl George proposed what has come to be called George's Buckets of Berries Theory (see fig. 6). His theory is an excellent help in understanding the nature of dominant coalitions. The theory was devised from an understanding of how berry farmers rotate berries to keep them fresh. To get a proper understanding of this theory, consider that you are involved in picking berries. Each day you go into a field, pick ripe berries, and bring them back to a shed. There you place the buckets of older berries on the left side of the shelf, to be used first, and the most recent buckets of berries on the right side of the shelf, to be used at a later time. Each day, you place the newer berries on the right and move the older berries to the left.

Figure 6

Carl George's Berry Bucket Theory

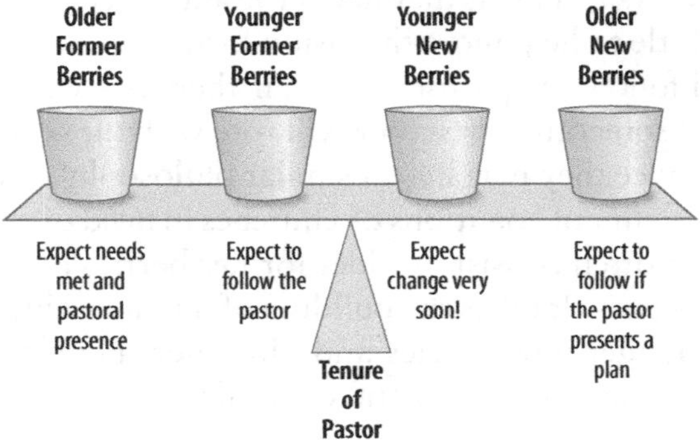

Older Former Berries	Younger Former Berries	Younger New Berries	Older New Berries
Expect needs met and pastoral presence	Expect to follow the pastor	Expect change very soon!	Expect to follow if the pastor presents a plan

Tenure of Pastor

Used by permission of Tom Harper and the Society for Church Consulting.

In a different context but similar manner, the people in a church can be described as former berries and new berries. The former berries are the people who have been in the church for some time, while the newcomers are the new berries. Naturally, new berries are placed on the right to be involved in the church at a later date—that is, if they remain long enough to become an older berry.

The former berries are composed of older former berries and their children, the younger former berries. New berries are made up of younger new berries—young persons, couples, and families—as well as older new berries, who usually are church transfers from other churches.

Dominant coalitions are most often composed of former berries, with the occasional addition of an older new berry. Younger new berries are kept out of church leadership positions until they are more mature and have less-radical ideas.

Older former berries view a new pastor as their personal caregiver and rarely are willing to follow his leadership in a new direction. The younger former berries may find the new pastor's ideas exciting, but when it comes time for a vote, they often side with their parents, the older former berries. After all, blood is thicker than water, and they will have to live with their parents after the pastor leaves. Younger new berries are on the pastor's side but, as they have little authority in the church, can do little to help move the vision forward. Older new berries will follow the pastor's vision if there is a well-designed plan, but sometimes even they will vote with the older former berries, since they may have a similar philosophy of ministry.

The dominant coalitions of churches in need of revitalization most often consist of older former berries and younger former berries. It takes the building of a new coalition made up of younger new berries and older new berries before a new vision can be implemented (see fig. 7).

Developing Your Coalition

For your church to be revitalized, you must form your own dominant coalition. The key question is how to replace the present dominant coalition without harming people. You have two options. One is to invite new people into the current

FIGURE 7

Carl George's Berry Bucket Theory

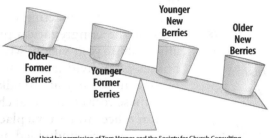

Used by permission of Tom Harper and the Society for Church Consulting.

dominant coalition. The second is to create a new dominant coalition.

In some cases, the first option is not possible. If the current dominant coalition is composed of one couple—a matriarch and a patriarch—there is no way to invite anyone onto that team. The same is true when the coalition is a group of families. You have to find some way to work around them, neutralize them, or outlive them. Each of these approaches is fraught with difficulty but should be considered. If the current dominant coalition is made up of an elected board, the nomination process may block new leaders from being selected. Policies that restrict participation on the board to members only, or at least to persons who have been in the church a number of years, serve to maintain the status quo.

Revitalizing a church normally means building a new coalition. Begin by recruiting a small group of the most committed and forward-thinking people to spearhead the revitalization effort. The following is a process by which you can identify future members of your new team.

First, resist the urge to preach about your vision from the pulpit. Also, do not hold a vote or congregational meeting or any other sort of meeting about the vision. It is too early. Doing so gives too much power and authority to any small negative power blocks, sometimes the old dominant coalition.

It will take only one negative person, family, or vote in some churches to kill the new vision before it even sees the light of day.

No one individual is ever able to develop the right vision, communicate it to large numbers of people, eliminate all the key obstacles, generate short-term wins, lead and manage dozens of change projects, and anchor new approaches deep in the organization's culture. Weak committees are even worse. A strong guiding coalition is always needed— one with the right composition, level of trust, and shared objective.

JOHN KOTTER

Second, begin meeting with members of the congregation individually to share your vision. Meet in the homes of individuals or at a quiet restaurant where you can talk. Never hold these conversations at church or in your office. You want a place where people can give undivided attention to what you are sharing as well as a place where they will feel comfortable asking questions.

Third, when you meet, ask individuals to share their vision for the future of the church. Listen attentively to whatever they have to say. Don't argue with them if they have ideas different from yours. Carefully take notes and watch their body language. When they finish sharing their understanding of the church's vision, tell them you have been giving this a great deal of thought and prayer, and ask if you can share what you see as the vision. They will almost assuredly say yes. Then share God's vision for the future, as you understand it, with them. Begin by explaining why things need to change and are going to change. Tell them exactly how things will be different. Paint as clear a picture of the new future of the church as possible.

Fourth, when you are finished, ask, "If our church moves in this direction, how could you see yourself participating?"

88

This is a very important question that will help you identify who should be a part of your new dominant coalition. If they can think of a way of helping, or if they clearly resonate with the vision, ask them to become a part of your team. Unfortunately, some (perhaps most) will not resonate, in which case thank them for their time, ask them to give it further thought, and close in prayer. Under no circumstances should disagreeable people be invited onto your team.

Fifth, begin meeting with your new dominant coalition for prayer, instruction, and planning. It may be wise to set a time early in the morning for your team to meet, say, 6:00 a.m. By doing so you will set a small hurdle for people to overcome, in this case, getting up early. Those who come will be committed to the vision and willing to invest serious effort in seeing it accomplished. Spend time talking about the vision, ways to overcome resistance, and plans to communicate it to the entire congregation.

Three Keys to a Successful Dominant Coalition

When you are talking with people and sharing your vision for the future of your church, keep the following three keys in mind. They are necessary for the new coalition to transform your church.

Recruit the right people.

Never recruit people for your new coalition publicly from the pulpit. If you do so, you will attract people who may not be a good fit for the team. By talking with people one-on-one, you are able to invite people you sense believe in the new vision and would work well with others. The number one criteria is a belief in the new vision, but the number two criteria is chemistry with the rest of the team. It is always helpful to have leaders on the coalition, or what some might call power players, meaning people who can make a difference in the church. But begin with the willing. Remember, if they want to run, run with them. If they want to walk, walk with them. If they want to sit, find someone else.

Require the right respect.

Trust is the primary power behind an effective coalition. Members should demonstrate respect for others on the team and be able to engage others in the church who may not agree with the new direction. If you know that some people do not work well with others, resist inviting them onto the team no matter how much in agreement they are with the vision. You don't have time to work on members' relationships on the coalition. Let them settle differences before being invited onto the team. Never invite those who are projects. Work on their personal or spiritual issues before involving them in the team. Recruit people who respect you. People buy into your vision when they buy into you. Again, invite people into the coalition only if they show loyalty to you and the office of pastor.

> *Teamwork is the ability to work together toward a common vision. It is the fuel that allows common people to attain uncommon results.*
> ANDREW CARNEGIE

Provide the right training.

Providence appears to favor the church with a plan over the one without one. So begin training the people on your coalition in the following areas. First, teach the biblical reason your church exists. Church consultant William Easum says, "Turnaround pastors . . . know that people need a spiritual foundation before they can understand why they must change. And change should always be for the sake of the gospel."[3] Build a biblical foundation so people understand God's hope for your church. Second, assist members of your new coalition to see the current reality of the church's situation. It is the leader's responsibility to help people grasp what is really going on.

Third, train members in change management and conflict management practices (see chap. 11). Revitalizing a church requires new practices and habits of ministry. A popular saying states, "If you keep doing what you've always done, you'll keep getting what you've always got." Unfortunately, it's worse. I've found that if people keep doing what they've always done, they'll actually get less than what they've always got. The reason? Every ministry has diminishing returns. So the practices of ministry that were fruitful ten or twenty or thirty years ago (sometimes longer) reach a point when they become less effective. Ministry must be renewed from time to time to keep it fresh. Refreshing a ministry creates changes, changes that are not always appreciated. Revitalization leaders expect and prepare people for conflict.

Replace Leaders

Begin building your new coalition quietly. As I mentioned before, don't announce it from the pulpit. Just start gathering new people one at a time. Meet with each newcomer who visits the church and share your burgeoning vision. Ask them if they could see themselves being a part of such a vision. If they say yes, invite them onto your new team.

Gradually, others in the church will begin to hear about your gathering and will start asking questions. Meet with them privately and share your growing vision of the future. Once again, ask them if they could see themselves being a part of your vision. Be careful not to invite disagreeable people. Remember the need for chemistry and for belief in the vision that is forming.

As openings on the board and other church organizations become available, try to appoint or elect someone from the new coalition. If you have a nominating committee, be sure to gain influence or control of that committee. At the least, as the pastor, you should have veto power over who is selected for any board, committee, or church position. This is no time to be modest or to take a backseat in nominating procedures. Do what is possible to bring new leaders into positions where they can make a difference in the church's long-term ministry.

CASE STUDY 6
Building a Dominant Coalition

After encountering major resistance from the church board regarding changes in the church ministry, Pastor Dennis Jacks realized he needed to build a new leadership team. He tried to get the congregation to elect some new members to the board but was always rebuffed with the statement, "They haven't been here long enough yet."

In desperation, Pastor Jacks and his wife, Janet, started meeting with individuals and couples privately. During the conversations, Pastor Jacks and Janet spoke openly about their dreams for the future of the church. As they painted a picture of a hopeful future, they noticed that some people's eyes literally opened wide. Of course, others just listened and showed little reaction.

Pastor Jacks and Janet believed that God had a remnant of people with whom they could start to rebuild the church. When they saw positive reactions among some of the people, they enthusiastically asked them to meet and pray together.

Occasionally, a new person or family visited the church, and Pastor Jacks and Janet would share their vision for the church with them too. Some newcomers were invited to join their growing team, which made the newcomers feel needed.

Slowly, Pastor Jacks began to notice that some of the people on his prayer team were rising to positions of leadership in the church. Without thinking about it, whenever there was a need for a new leader, worker, or committee member in the church, he just naturally suggested someone from the prayer

team. Over time, those in leadership were people who understood his vision and were loyal to his leadership in the church.
It took about five years for this to happen, as people moved
naturally out of different positions and new people came into
the church. Eventually, Pastor Jacks and Janet noticed that
the conflicts over the direction of the church were diminishing. The new leaders owned the new vision and were willing to
make changes to take the church in a new direction.

Analysis:

- How did Pastor Jacks and his wife build a new coalition?
- What was the natural outgrowth of the new coalition over
  time?
- What was the process Pastor Jacks used to communicate
  the vision?

Bringing It Home

1. What is the makeup of your church's present dominant coalition? Are those on the
   coalition the right people to help you revitalize the church?

2. Who in the church resonates with your God-given vision of the future? Are they willing
   to join with you in prayer and planning for the future?

3. Who are the older berries and the new berries? Make a list of all those in the church
   using the four categories of berries noted in this chapter. After making the list, think
   through what it means for your revitalization efforts. What insights can you gain
   from such an analysis?

4. How can you begin this week to build a new dominant coalition to assist in revitalizing
   your church?

Lift the Morale

You have to give up "I can't."
JACK CANFIELD

Some years ago, George Barna noted that one of the differences between growing and nongrowing churches is attitude.[1] His, as well as others', research posits that growing churches believe they have something to give—the good news of Jesus Christ—to their surrounding communities. This belief builds a positive morale among the congregants and helps them believe their church is important to the city in which it is located. Positive morale leads to positive energy to reach out and grow.

If you want to see your church revitalized, you have to help the congregation give up "I can't" statements, as well as other comments such as, "We're just a small church." Comments like these disempower a church, making it weaker than it really is. A church's corporate attitude drives its actions.

Evaluating Church Morale

How is your church's morale? Does your church believe it has something of value to offer its people? Community? City? Listening to your people and observing their actions can help you determine morale. To paraphrase a well-known statement from the Bible, "He who has an ear to hear, or an eye to see, listen and observe." The following points will help you begin listening to your people to determine their morale.

Ask direct questions.

Whenever you have the opportunity, ask your leaders, classes, and small groups some of the following questions: How do you feel about our church? What do you hear others saying about our church? Are you proud of our church? If so, what makes you proud? If not, what makes you embarrassed?

Listen passively to others.

When you are attending church activities or participating in fellowship times, what do you hear people say about your church? Are they excited about your church? Do you hear discouraging comments? Is the tone of their conversations positive or negative?

Take complaints seriously.

If you are like many church leaders, you get complaints almost weekly. After hearing complaints on a regular basis, you may have a tendency to log them away like an old email and forget about them. This may be a mistake. Complaints carry tones of morale. Not only listen to what is being complained about but also try to hear the frustration, embarrassment, or discouragement within the complaint. If complaints include overtones or undertones of anger, it almost certainly means a negative attitude exists in the church.

Catalog what leaders say to the congregation.

What do you hear other leaders saying to the congregation or in classes and small groups? Is the tone of comments positive or negative? Leaders reflect the attitudes of the people they lead, and people reflect the attitudes of the people who lead them. What attitudes are reflected by your leaders?

Observe nonverbal behavior.

Are congregants taking pride in the ministry? How do they care for the building and grounds? Are people chronically late to events? Do they invite their friends, family members, or colleagues to church events? These things and others demonstrate pride of ownership or lack of such pride. What does the nonverbal behavior of your people say about morale in your church?

When analyzing your church's morale, be sure to take into consideration your people. Some may just be negative, while others are perpetually happy. Check out your perceptions with others in the church to see if they are sensing the same attitudes or if you are misinterpreting impressions. Feedback is an important aspect of interpreting the morale of your church.

Strategies for Building Morale

People get tired of struggling. The constant battle to survive takes its toll on a congregation. One step in the process of revitalization is to lift the morale of the people. Here are some practical ideas you can use to build a new sense of esteem in your congregation.

Be positive yourself.

People take cues from leaders. When leaders are positive, seeing the glass half-full rather than half-empty, people begin to think in a positive manner as well (see fig. 8). Follow the example of Jesus, who saw beyond the disciples' problems and invested in their possibilities. See the good in people, pay attention to their potential, and bless the best. Speak well of others (people or churches). As mothers always say, "If you can't say anything nice, don't say anything at all." As you practice this policy, people will begin to believe it too. Monitor your language to make certain it sets a good tone about the church. Show your ownership and care for the church by keeping your office neat, picking up trash, and being on time for meetings.

FIGURE 8
Half-Full or Half-Empty?

Find the silver lining.

As common wisdom predicts, even the darkest cloud has a silver lining. Every situation, no matter how dire, has its good aspects. Find the positive in your situation and highlight it. Speak about the good, the hopeful, and the excellent. Find the good that is happening in your church and call attention to it. Thank people who are overworked, praise past accomplishments, noting that God is still doing good things today, and be sure to focus on prayers of thanksgiving. Talk about the church's strengths, not weaknesses.

Celebrate all victories.

If you review Old Testament history, you'll find that, as one person put it, "God loves a party." God commanded that his people hold feasts and celebrations as a way of reminding them of his love and care. Israel was to practice these events even when they were in difficult situations. As you work to revitalize your church, keep the same idea in mind. Whenever you have the smallest of triumphs, celebrate them. When you put on a new coat of paint in the auditorium, celebrate it. When a guest shows up due to the invitation of a worshiper, celebrate it. When you meet the budget for the month, celebrate it. Take every opportunity to praise people's hard work, effort, and accomplishments. Remember that little victories lead to large triumphs.

Employ hopeful language.

If you are a smaller church, do not downplay your size. Instead of saying, "We're a small church," say, "We're a typical-size church." Using this type of language allows you to recast the church in a positive light. The typical church has a lot to offer. Talk about opportunities rather than problems. Speak of challenges instead of limitations. Banish the word *failure* but give voice to the word *experiment*. Whenever a new experiment does not work, tell the people you now know of another way that does not work. Experiments very often do not work out as planned, but they lead to ideas that work in the future. When a person told Thomas Edison he was a failure at creating an electric lightbulb, he reportedly replied, "I'm not a failure. I now know one thousand ways not to do it!" Take that same attitude in your church. Never, never, never accept defeat. If you try something new and it does not pan out as you expected, try again.

Change the rules.

When people approach you with a problem, ask them to come back later with three possible solutions. Shut out the naysayers by establishing a new rule in meetings that negative comments must come with three positive alternatives. This will cause leaders to look for the positives and gradually help to change the atmosphere. It takes ten positive comments to overcome one negative one, so work hard at eliminating negative responses.

Recruit encouragers.

Find the people who are positive thinkers and give them opportunities to be cheerleaders. Allow those who see the possibilities to give testimonies, share during worship, and speak out during decision-making times. They will lift and encourage others, helping you to build the morale of the entire congregation.

Highlight your heroes.

Applaud those in your church who are making positive contributions to the ministry. Establish an award for those who serve above and beyond the call of duty. Name the award after a well-known saint in your church who served faithfully, or give it a silly name like the "Golden Banana Award." When you highlight the heroes, they serve as role models for others in the congregation. As people begin to emulate the heroes, morale rises.

Turn negative comments in positive directions.

Churches attract hurting people who are looking for love. Unfortunately, hurting people hurt others by extending their own poor self-images onto the church. Channel comments from negative people in a positive direction by listening to what they say and then rewording their complaint toward the positive. For example, a complaint like, "I couldn't find a parking space today," becomes, "Isn't it wonderful that God is bringing us so many new people?" A complaint like, "We don't have enough workers," becomes, "Isn't it wonderful that we have a few dedicated workers?"

Find ways to serve others.

People always tend to find the greatest happiness in helping others. I was watching television during the Thanksgiving holiday and enjoyed the interviews with people who were serving food at shelters and inner-city missions. As people talked to the reporter, they all said in one way or another that serving others brought them joy. If you want a surefire way to raise the morale of people in your church, find a way to get them involved in serving someone less fortunate. Maybe you could find a widow who needs her house painted and take it on as a church-wide project. People will forget their own problems as they focus on creative ways to raise money to buy paint, work together painting the house, and see the thankfulness in the face of the homeowner. Morale will go up as they reach out to others in love and compassion. Give people a way to feel good about themselves and their church.

Follow the church's long-term passion.

Most churches in need of revitalization had a better day. Find out what sparked the church's early passion during the days gone by and build on that passion again. For instance, during one church's heyday, it focused on ministry to children through a camp program. The church's passion was for evangelism of children, not camping. So to raise morale, the church began highlighting its long-term love for children. All churches have a natural DNA, so find the passion embedded in your church's DNA and bring it to the front once again.

Help people succeed.

One of my all-time favorite stories comes from Elmer Towns. As I remember the story, he was pastoring his first church and determined that the sanctuary needed repainting. When he brought the idea to the small congregation, he discovered resistance due to the small budget of the church.

In a moment of inspiration, he picked up a piece of white chalk and walked over to a wall in the sanctuary. Standing on his tiptoes, he reached as high as possible and drew a chalk line straight down to the floor. Then he walked about ten feet along the wall and reached up and drew another line down to the floor. He then turned and called one man by name, asking him if his family could afford to buy one gallon of paint and then come to church one day and paint the ten-foot area between the two lines. Caught off guard, the man replied, "Yes." Immediately, Dr. Towns returned to the wall and wrote the man's name on the wall between the two lines. Then he walked farther along the wall and drew another line down to the floor. He turned to the congregation again and called on another family, asking them if they could afford to buy one bucket of paint and come to church and paint the area between the next two lines. Following the lead of the first family, they said, "Yes." Again Dr. Towns returned to the wall and wrote their name in chalk between the next two lines. Dr. Towns continued this procedure until he went entirely around the inner walls of the sanctuary. After determining the color and type of paint, the congregation purchased paint and did the work. The sanctuary got a new coat of paint, and everyone felt good about the project. As you might imagine, morale went up. When you help people succeed, you will see their morale rise.

Stay close to the people.

You may not want to admit it. In fact, you may have been told it is not true. But all things being equal, people feel good about things when they know they are loved. If people in your church perceive that you care about them, they will feel better about themselves and their church. Churches that are in need of revitalization are quite often composed of hurting people. You can capture their attention by remaining humble. Raising morale does not require a rah-rah type of leadership. Quiet confidence is attractive and makes people feel at ease. During conversations, say less and ask more questions. Then lean forward and really listen. Express genuine enjoyment in being with others and always be willing to laugh. Be well intentioned and well mannered and share compliments generously.

People will believe what you say when they believe in you. Once you have their attention, they will begin to believe what you say and feel about the church. With so many messages directed to people each day—through emails, spam, advertising, infomercials, television commercials, radio ads—people are skeptical. They are much more willing to believe people they know and like. When people like the source of a message, they tend to trust the message. Staying close to the people builds credibility.

Focus on the very important people.

There are at least four groups of people who will engage your time in church ministry. The first group is the VIPs, or the Very Important People. These are the leaders who will help bring about revitalization in the church ministry. If they are not already in key ministry positions in your church, you should work to place them in those positions as quickly as possible.

The second group is the VTPs, or the Very Trainable People. Some people show potential for leadership, but they are not yet ready. They are the people you should be mentoring each week and with whom you should be sharing your vision and hopes for the future.

The third group is the VNPs, or the Very Nice People. For the most part, these people are not now nor ever will be leaders of the church. Yet, they are loyal to you and the vision you have for the church. Since they cause no trouble and generally are supportive of all church ministries, they are nice folks to serve.

The fourth group is the VDPs, or the Very Draining People. They are barriers to your efforts at revitalization and cause great pain to those who desire improved vitality in the church.

Jesus was surrounded by the same four groups during his earthly ministry. The twelve disciples were the VIPs, the seventy were the VTPs, the crowds were the VNPs, and the Pharisees and Sadducees were the VDPs. With which group did he spend the greatest amount of time? The VIPs—the twelve disciples. In whom did he invest the least amount of time? The VDPs—the Pharisees and Sadducees.

As you work to revitalize your church, you must decide where to invest your time. All four of these groups will want you to be with them. Revitalization pastors tend to spend time with the VDPs because they demand to be heard. However, revitalization leaders spend time with the VIPs and the VTPs, preferring to invest in those who will prove helpful in the process of revitalization.

CASE STUDY 7
Lifting Morale

Living Waters Church was only twenty years old, but it was showing signs of a much older church. The rapid growth that took place in its first four years was quickly smothered when the founding pastor left. During the following four years, two pastors came and went in rapid succession. This effectively put the church on a long-term plateau lasting nearly its entire life.

After accepting a call to Living Waters, Pastor Frazer found a church family with a defeated spirit. He knew that attitudes drive the action of a church, which was obvious at Living Waters. Members greeted each other with a sort of "poor us" attitude. Nothing, it seemed, had ever worked at Living Waters. The church felt its only calling was to give young pastors right out of seminary their first experience. They knew from experience, and actually expected, young pastors to quickly move on to a better church after gaining a bit of experience at Living Waters. Their expectations became a self-fulfilling prophecy.

A total of eight pastors had come and gone, none staying more than four years. Pastor Frazer knew he would have to stay longer than that before people would begin to believe in him, but he also realized something had to be done to raise morale.

After prayer and much thinking, he determined to work diligently to improve morale. He put into place the following plan of action:

- Remind the people of how much they love and care for one another.
- Focus sermons on faith, hope, and love.
- Praise the people for staying faithful to God and his church.
- Celebrate anything and everything as a means of bringing back positive feelings among the people.
- Generate short-term wins by doing two or three small projects and then celebrating the accomplishments.

Pastor Frazer felt this strategy would raise the corporate self-esteem of the congregation during his first year while building a small foundation of positive feelings that he could build upon for the next.

Analysis:

- What past experiences at Living Waters Church led to the low morale of the congregation?
- What did Pastor Frazer do to help raise the morale?
- What principles do you see in this case study that might help you and your church?

Bringing It Home

1. How is your church's morale? Give some specific examples that support your view.

2. What are you doing or what can you do to raise morale this week? This month? This year?

3. Where are you investing the bulk of your time? Is it with your VIPs, VTPs, VNPs, or VDPs?

4. How can you begin to invest more time with your VIPs and VTPs?

8

Make Hard Decisions

Church Revitalization Chart

See the Potential

Commit to Lead

Assess the Situation

Learn the Principles

Discern God's Vision

Build a Coalition

Lift the Morale

Make Hard Decisions

Refocus the Ministry

Equip for Change

Deal with Resistance

Stay the Course

Breaking Through

If you have to eat a pondful of frogs, eat the large frogs first.

ANONYMOUS

Revitalizing a church sometimes calls for drastic changes. This is similar to what happens in corporate America when changes must be made in order for a company to thrive or even survive. For example, a few years ago General Motors Corporation faced the reality of declining sales by filing for Chapter 11 bankruptcy protection. Once one of the largest and most productive corporations in the United States, General Motors made the difficult decisions to sell off four lines of automobiles, close nine manufacturing plants, and cut forty thousand hourly and twenty-three thousand salaried employees. GM's stock fell to a low of twenty-seven cents per share. By making the hard decisions, the company created a customer-focused, leaner, and decisive structure, which became competitive in the marketplace. Two years later the company was profitable, and GM's stock was trading at $34.26.[1]

Churches seldom change without a strong environmental shock triggered by technological, economic, or social pressures. For churches to thrive, decisive leaders willing to make difficult decisions must meet these shocks. Such challenges often release energy for revitalization. But if leaders are not decisive and willing to make hard choices, such challenges may also release organizational and personal resistance.

Eat the Big Frogs First

For several years, one of my fellow professors had an interesting sign on his office door. Around a large picture of different-sized frogs sitting on lily pads in a pond, it read, "How do you eat a group of frogs? Eat the big ones first!" Whenever students had several projects due around the same time, they used to ask him how to prioritize their work. The sign was his way of saying to do the big projects—or the most difficult ones—first.

It's safe to say that revitalization leaders eat the big frogs first. In other words, they make the hardest decisions first. One thing that most researchers agree on is that revitalization leaders are decisive. Some pastors desire to see revitalization take place while keeping everyone already in the church happy. This leads them to neglect making difficult decisions. When pastors see what must be done but are unable or unwilling to make the hard decisions necessary to revitalize the church, there will be a slow, continual decline.

There are three major decisions that revitalization leaders must make to turn churches around.

Cut the fat.

Oftentimes, a church in decline was once much larger. As churches grow, they naturally add staff and programs and spend greater amounts of money. Then when the church begins declining, the leaders attempt to keep doing everything the church did when it was much larger. Gradually, the church finds itself with fewer resources trying to support too many programs, many now unproductive. Revitalization leaders make the hard decisions to cut programs, lay off staff, and narrow the focus of ministry. The bottom line is you must stop the hemorrhaging. All churches in need of renewal have one or more ministries that are not fruitful. With limited resources of people, energy, and finances, you can't continue to do everything the church has been doing.

> *You need a plan to live. If you don't make it through the storm, the rest doesn't matter.*
> JIM COLLINS

To accomplish more, try doing less. Narrow your focus and reduce your programs (those not honestly needed). With key leaders, make a list of all the ministries and programs your church conducts. Underline the ones that are absolutely needed. What *must* your church continue to do? If possible, eliminate the rest and begin all over.

Control the cash.

Revitalization leaders take personal responsibility to have an up-to-the-minute awareness of income and disbursements. This is contrary to what is taught in seminary. Future pastors are normally advised to keep out of the finances of a church as much as possible. But when a church is in decline, particularly those in a desperate situation, finances become a crucial aspect of staying alive long enough to see revitalization take root. Thus, revitalization leaders keep their eyes on the finances of the church and make disbursements sparingly.

They insist on weekly financial updates to keep on top of the money flow.

Revitalization leaders know the exact amount of money needed each week and month for the church to remain solvent. This translates into knowing three key figures: fixed expenses, general expenses, and income. Fixed expenses are what the church absolutely must pay out each month to remain open. They include items such as salary, mortgage (rent or lease), taxes, and utilities. General expenses are additional money the church needs to do ministry. They include items such as curriculum purchases, advertising, landscaping expenses, and facility upkeep. Income, of course, is the amount of money given to the church through tithes and offerings, rents, or interest received.

One way to visualize the financial situation of a church is to use a picture similar to the one in figure 9.

Figure 9
Income and Expenses

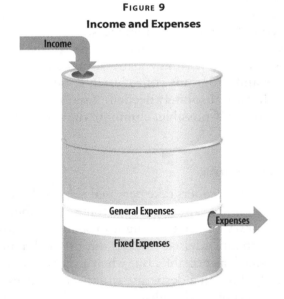

Visualize the income of the church being poured into a barrel. Near the bottom of the barrel is a hole out of which money flows when spent on fixed and general expenses. Revitalization leaders know how much they must have (fixed expenses) to stay afloat as a church and how much they need to do a basic ministry (general expenses). They monitor the income weekly and monthly so they know the exact financial shape the church is in at any moment. In desperate situations, it is wise to pay only items that are absolutely necessary, meaning fixed expenses. Pay in this order only those bills that will keep the church open: payroll, mortgage, utilities, and taxes. As extra money is available, continue to pay ministry expenses in this order: worship, children, and outreach/evangelism.

The hard decisions are related to whom to lay off and which ministries to eliminate or at least stop supporting. In general, it is best to keep people who are the most fruitful and valuable in reaching new people and the ministries that serve potential newcomers from the community, usually worship and children's ministries. It does no good to cut outreach and evangelism programs, as they are the main source of potential growth and vitality.

Making difficult financial decisions puts everyone on alert that there are no sacred cows and that you are a leader who can and will make the tough decisions.

Confront problem people.

Few pastors enjoy confronting others, but motion always creates friction. When a church begins to move in a new direction, problem people will appear. In churches that experience a lack of leadership, difficult people emerge to take charge. When fresh leadership comes along, such people find it difficult to relinquish control.

One of the best examples of this is what took place when Nehemiah arrived to take over the rebuilding of the wall in Jerusalem. Problem people immediately emerged in the persons of Sanballat and Tobiah (see Neh. 4). Their opposition started with only verbal disagreement but escalated into anger and outright physical attack. At first, Nehemiah simply ignored them. When the opposition grew worse, Nehemiah called the people to prayer and set up guards for protection from possible assaults. Eventually, Nehemiah was forced to confront Tobiah (see Neh. 13).

In a revitalization ministry, it is wise to confront sooner rather than later. So confront when necessary. The key is the word *necessary*. In general, it is best to confront those who

- are disloyal: people who on the surface appear to be with you but speak against you when you are not present
- are belligerent: people who verbally or physically attack others
- belittle: people who put others down in an effort to make themselves look better
- threaten: people who say they will resign or speak to others but don't
- undermine: people who seek to draw others away to create a new church

Accept any and all resignations immediately whenever someone threatens to leave. Thank them for their service but accept the resignation. This often catches them off guard, since they most likely have used this tactic before. Once you accept their resignation, do not back down and do not allow the person to change his or her mind.

Face your fears. Do what you should do—today. Don't put things off. Pastors tend to shy away from confronting others, hoping things will change. This rarely happens, and they end up putting off the confrontation longer than necessary while allowing the problem person to keep making trouble. Remember, short-term gain leads to long-term pain, while short-term pain leads to long-term gain.

Making Hard Decisions

Ocean Shore Church was nearly dead. At least that's how Pastor Shapira read the situation. After taking stock of the church's condition, he concluded that immediate action was necessary if the church was to survive long enough even to think about revitalizing.

When he met with the leaders to discuss the first steps of revitalizing the church, he took charge and laid out an action plan that called for some drastic measures. The leaders had indicated their desperation, and one of the elders had said, "Pastor, we don't want to die, so just tell us what to do." Pastor Shapira took them at their word. He was telling them what to do.

He told the board clearly that difficult decisions had to be made regarding programs, finances, and refocusing of the ministry. He insisted that the church treasurer provide a weekly update on the income and all payables and that he, the pastor, would approve any and all expenditures. In addition, he insisted on getting an update every Monday morning concerning weekly attendance figures for worship and all children's programs from the head usher. These requests, or rather requirements, caused a small stir among the head usher and the treasurer, but both finally agreed they could provide the weekly reports by Monday morning.

However, it was what came next that caused the major furor. He said that the Christian high school the church had been running for the last thirty years had to be closed. The school was losing money, and the church had to cover the losses. Pastor Shapira expressed regret over having to close this ministry but said it had to be done.

This caught the board by surprise, and Mr. Bob Foster sputtered, "If you close the school, I'll resign," whereupon Pastor Shapira replied, "Bob, I'm sorry you feel that way, but we are closing the school and I accept your resignation."

113

With those words, Mr. Foster became flustered and commented, "I didn't really mean it. I don't want to leave the board." But Pastor Shapira gave no ground. "I'm sorry, Bob, but you resigned, and I accepted your resignation. You are no longer on the board."

The remainder of the board members sat in disbelief. They had seen Bob Foster threaten to resign before, but this was the first time a pastor had the courage to take him up on his offer. They all realized it was a new day at Ocean Shore.

Analysis:

- In what ways did Pastor Shapira make the hard decisions?
- How did he handle the disagreement of his board members?
- Do you think he made the right decisions? Why or why not?

Lyle Schaller once noted that only around 20 percent of church pastors should change nothing in the first year.[2] This is especially true of pastors serving churches in need of revitalization. Churches that have struggled through a change of pastors, a loss of attendees, and a loss of reputation in a community need immediate leadership. The old idea of taking a year to get to know the people before doing anything is unwise. Holding down the fort for a while is a deadly approach when people are looking for someone to lead them in love.

Face reality as it is, not as it was or as you wish it were. You cannot turn a church around with half measures. Be sure to go far enough. Half measures will give you less than halfway results. The key word is *proactive*. Control your destiny or someone or something else will. Make the hard decisions, and while you're at it, eat the largest frogs first.

114

Bringing It Home

1. Do you find it difficult or easy to make hard decisions regarding church ministry? Which types of decisions are the most difficult for you to make? Which are the easiest?

2. Are you facing difficult decisions right now in your church? What is holding you back from making them?

3. Do you know how much cash your church needs each month to keep functioning? Are you receiving weekly updates on the income, fixed expenses, and general expenses? Why not?

4. Are there people you need to confront but are unwilling to face? What are your fears? What will be the long-term results if you continue to put off talking with them? What is the worse that could happen if you talked to them this week?

9

Refocus the Ministry

People are more receptive to outreach from new groups and classes than from long-established groups and classes.

GEORGE G. HUNTER III

As many stories begin, once upon a time an old man purchased a long-neglected piece of property. It was rough and ugly, littered with weeds and thorns. On the property was a tiny rock house—broken, sagging, cracking, leaking. The old man worked on the property for five long years, and under his loving care it became a showplace. The garden was magnificent. The tiny house was cheery and inviting. People visited to relax in the garden, enjoy the sparkling pools, gaze upon the beautiful flowerbeds, and rest for a while in the comfort of the little house. One day a friend who hadn't seen the old man in many years came by for a visit.

117

He walked around the property absolutely enthralled. "This is beautiful! Absolutely magnificent! Simply fantastic! Isn't it marvelous to view the handiwork of God?"

"Humph!" snorted the old man. "You should have seen it when God worked it alone."

God, of course, can do his work alone. Yet he chooses not to do so. He called Abram, Moses, David, Nehemiah, John the Baptist, Peter, Paul, and, yes, us too to share in his work. Beautiful gardens do not happen without work—tilling the soil, fertilizing, planting, watering, weeding, spraying for insects. God's handiwork in gardens or churches becomes beautiful with the help of God's people. The Great Commission can also be called the Great Co-mission, since it is God's and ours. As we engage in his work, he will always be with us.

Clock Builders instead of Time Tellers

God has told us the *what*, "Go therefore and make disciples." It is up to us to determine the *how*. While he has declared the *direction*, we must provide the *plans*. For some reason, however, leaders in pleateaued and declining churches find it difficult to develop workable plans. They find it easier to adopt what another church is doing. Church leaders have borrowed and successfully used programs from other churches for years. Sometimes this works very well. We don't always have to reinvent the wheel. But we all know that sometimes the way another church does a ministry doesn't always work in our church. In most situations, it is better to *adapt* a ministry rather than just *adopt* it.

In this sense, we need to be clock builders rather than time tellers. This idea was first advanced by James Collins in his book *Built to Last: Successful Habits of Visionary Companies*. Clock building is focused on the uniqueness of what God wants for your church. Time telling is placing a focus on one innovative idea another church is doing that

118

may be right for a time. In business, time-telling companies have focused on buggy whips, large gas-guzzling cars, catalog sales, and a host of other ideas that worked for a time. Time-telling churches have focused on bus ministry, direct mail advertising, or seeker-centered ministry. Of course, all ideas, programs, or ministries were innovative in the beginning. But each was originally designed for a particular church in a specific cultural situation to meet a verifiable need. Later, other churches copy programs without considering the cultural or ministry fit. Thus, churches become time tellers rather than clock builders.

Yes, some churches borrow great ideas that are working right now, but will they be right in the future? Build a church that has the capacity to outlive one idea. Focus on clock building rather than time telling. Here are some ideas on how to get started.

Give your church a checkup.

Each year I go to my doctor for an annual checkup. The nurse determines my height, eyesight, weight, and blood pressure. The laboratory checks the sugar level in my blood. Based on these quantitative statistics, the doctor makes a qualitative judgment as to how healthy I am.

In the same manner, analyze the statistics of your church. You need to know how long your church has been on its present decline or plateau. It will be helpful to discover the causes and traumas behind the church's plunge into decline. As you look at the statistics, ask why ups and downs occurred. Seek to discover why the church got where it is today.

Interview long-term attendees to obtain insights as to what went on in the past. Pastor Barry Campbell suggests, "A discussion of the successes and failures of the past might save a lot of wasted effort. Some of those church members who have resisted growth might strongly support the efforts of a pastor who took the time to ask for their help in

119

interpreting the past."[1] Seek to discover any significant barriers, circumstances, or issues that have plagued the church over the years.

Investigate the community.

Carefully look at the community where your church is located. Is the population growing or declining? What is the average age of people in the community? What is the ethnic makeup? What is the socioeconomic level of the people near your church?

Once you pull together this essential information, compare it to your own church. How does your church compare to what you see in the community? Is there a close match or a mismatch?

Evaluate your ministries.

Bring your board or dominant coalition together and list all your church ministries. Then ask, "If we were starting from scratch today, what would we do? What would we not do?" As people glance over the list, circle the ministries they feel they would do and cross out the ones they think they wouldn't do. As an exercise, look at the ministries from a real church in case study 9. If you were starting a church today, which ministries would you do? Based on what you discover, what does it all mean for your church? What current programs or ministries need to be changed? Adapted? Replaced? What needs are there in the community that are appropriate for your church to meet?

CASE STUDY 9
What Ministries Would You Start Today?

worship	long-range planning team	Angel Tree
women's Bible study	publicity committee	midweek Bible study
senior high youth group	ushers	prayer committee
Awana	elder board	annual meeting
Thanksgiving supper	Alpha team	missions committee

campus security and safety	membership team	Christian education board
drama ministry	Saturday night service	visitor follow-up
church library	fellowship committee	website
church newsletter	adult choir	church directory
maintenance team	janitorial service	men's breakfast
homeless ministry	welcome team	worship team
October harvest festival	floral committee	computer support
trustee board	baptism committee	school commission
college ministry	career fellowship	inner-city renewal team
audiovisual committee	deaconess board	women's missionary union
home visitation	counseling ministry	landscape maintenance
parking team	finance committee	missionary committee
MOPS	communion	nominating committee
vacation Bible school	local evangelism	wedding committee
Sunday school	nursing home ministry	discipleship ministry
advisory committee	social committee	short-term missions
jail ministry	sports ministry	small group program
deacon board	leadership development	morning prayer group
community events	preschool program	
	Christian day school	

Examine the focus of your church.

Start with an evaluation of the finances of your church. Take the annual budget and break it down into major parts, such as education, missions, facility, personnel, local evangelism/outreach, and mortgage. Determine the percentage of each major part of the budget. Where is the money focused? If you are like most churches, the major focus of the finances is in providing salaries and benefits for the church personnel: pastor, secretary, etc. This is normal, but the major issue is how much is being used on outreach and evangelism in your local community. For a church to be revitalized, it needs to focus a minimum of 5 percent of its entire budget on local outreach and evangelism.

Next, examine the ministry focus of your church. First, make a list of every ministry or program in which your church is currently engaged. Second, on another piece of paper, write the following three words across the top in large letters: evangelism, assimilation, and education. Last, list each ministry under

121

these words. List all the evangelism ministries under the word *evangelism*, all the programs that help assimilate newcomers into your church under *assimilation*, and all the ministries that help your people grow spiritually under *education*.

After doing this exercise, look at the page and ask, What is the focus of our church? You can tell the focus of a church by evaluating where the money and the ministry time are spent. How much focus is on outreach and evangelism? How much time, money, and energy is directed inward on current church members versus people outside the church?

The Power of Focus

A friend of mine once wrote, "The person with focus is the person with the authority. When a person has focus, it provides leverage to influence others." This is true when attempting to revitalize a church. In some ways, just focusing on something—anything—is the beginning of turning around a plateaued or declining situation. Yet, it's best to focus on something that provides real direction rather than expending energy just for the sake of doing something.

Refocus on your core ministry.

After studying your church and community, ask your leaders, "What sets us apart from other churches? What can our church offer to the community that is uniquely us?" To find your unique identity, find out what God is already blessing. Categorize all your church ministries by the following titles:

- stars: the most fruitful ministries—that is, the ones that are responsible for bringing in the most new people or reaching the most people for Christ. If you cannot find any ministries that have proven effective in reaching new people, identify the ones that appear to have the greatest potential for doing so.

122

- puzzles: the ministries that appear to be good but are not producing the results you think they should.
- plow horses: the popular ministries that do not result in many new people coming to Christ or your church but which you must keep.
- dogs: the ministries that are draining your church of resources and produce almost no results. Deal with dogs by retooling them, reinventing them, or replacing them with stars.

If you find you have no stars, refocus by starting one new ministry a year for the next five years. It is a well-established fact that new ministries reach new people. If you seriously wish to reach new people, you must start something new. Programs and ministries become less effective with age. New ministries are the most fruitful.

Refocus on outreach and evangelism.

Contrary to popular thought, there is a difference between outreach and evangelism. Both are important to revitalizing a church, but it is helpful to think about the differences.

Outreach is any activity that serves to build a relationship with people in a church's community. This can be accomplished without actually talking about Christ or the gospel. Service projects, such as painting a widow's house, cleaning up a neighborhood park, or handing out cold water on a hot day, are all outreach activities. Such activities help the church develop a presence of love and care in the community.

Evangelism, on the other hand, is any activity that serves to proclaim the gospel of salvation in Jesus Christ and to persuade people to accept Christ as their personal Savior. Such activities help the church win new converts to Christ and his church.

Plateaued and declining churches regularly discover that they have little money, personnel, or ministry activities focused on outreach and evangelism. To revitalize a church, it is necessary to refocus on these activities.

Refocusing the Church

Revitalization leaders typically do one or more of the following in the process of refocusing their church.

Refocus reports on the future.

Nearly all churches have an end-of-the-year meeting at which people present reports on the past year's activities. Revitalization leaders find it helpful to refocus such reports on the future. Church leaders give reports on how they are going to reach out to newcomers. For example, the women's missionary group might present a report on how they hope to increase the number of women involved in their group.

Designate budget for outreach.

Refocus by designating 5 percent of your total budget for local outreach and evangelism, and then spend it on activities to reach out to the community. For example, copies of the *Jesus* film might be purchased and delivered to five hundred homes around the church. Or an attractive website might be designed to communicate to people outside the church.

Offer evangelism training for church attendees.

Offer friendship evangelism classes to church attendees. Ask each participant to make a list of non-Christian people they know who live near the church, to pray for them, and to build a relationship with them over the coming year. Training 10 percent of the congregation each year for five years is best. Within five years you'll have trained 50 percent of the congregation in how to build friendships for Christ, and that will make a noticeable difference in the church's attitudes toward newcomers.

Redirect ministries for outreach.

Think about how old programs can be refocused for outreach. For example, you might recast your Thanksgiving fellowship meal as a harvest festival and invite people from the community to take part.

Offer quarterly outreach events.

Offer one event each quarter that reaches out to the community. For instance, you could offer a weekend seminar on financial management. Encourage church members, who have been praying for nonchurched friends and family members, to bring people to these events.

CASE STUDY 10
Refocusing Church Ministry

After discovering that Faith Redeemer Church was in serious decline, Rev. Schmidt decided it might be worthwhile to go through old church records to see what past events had brought about the church's dreadful situation.

On the determined day, he blew the dust from the church filing cabinet and spent a morning reading through old church records of congregational and board business meetings. One issue sprang from the records that he had not noticed previously. There had not been a single adult baptism in the last twelve years.

Upon reflection, he recalled something a professor in seminary had emphasized some years before: new ministries are needed for evangelism to take place. This truth was never more obvious than at Faith Redeemer. Not only had there been no adult baptisms in the last twelve years, but there had been no new programs or ministries started during the past twenty years or more. From all appearances, the church had reached a peak of fruitfulness over two decades ago and then had stopped initiating any new ministries. The results had been predictable.

Even worse, from Rev. Schmidt's perspective, was that the church had no ministry programs aimed at the nonchurched. Not only were church ministries stagnant, but they were also all targeted toward those already in the church.

With this knowledge in hand, Rev. Schmidt embarked on a plan to refocus the church's priorities on the nonchurched community. To begin, he initiated the assistance of a church member who owned a printing business. Together they developed a plan to blanket the community in a five-mile radius of the church with brochures about the church. They didn't expect to get a lot of visitors from these mailings, but they hoped to raise the visibility of the church in the minds of its neighbors.

That same year Rev. Schmidt encouraged another church member to begin a weeknight children's outreach modeled on popular scouting programs. Since the church member had prior scouting experience, he agreed to be the leader of this new program. Advertising was prepared and distributed in parks and at local stores near the church.

To begin refocusing church members' thoughts on those outside the church, Rev. Schmidt preached a six-part series on loving your neighbor and initiated a new class called "Making Friends for Jesus." He personally recruited fifteen people to attend.

Finally, he met with the women's group to see if they would be willing to refocus the Thanksgiving celebration, which was always held on the Wednesday evening before Thanksgiving. With his encouragement, the event was changed to a harvest festival specifically aimed at attracting the community. One of the church members, a local elementary school teacher, had her children bake small pumpkin pies to donate to the event.

The children then asked their parents to go to the harvest festival to see and eat the pies they had made the day before.

The church's hard work of refocusing its ministry resulted in an increase in worship attendance. During the year, the church added seventeen new worshipers. As newcomers became more frequent at worship, morale improved and additional ministry programs were added to reach the community in the following year.

Analysis:

- What led to Rev. Schmidt's insights?
- How did he refocus the church's ministry outward?
- What can you learn from Rev. Schmidt's experience at Faith Redeemer Church?

Follow the ninety-second rule. How many times do ideas pop into your mind but you don't do anything about them? Ideas without execution amount to . . . well, diddly-squat. What makes an idea successful is not the idea. Ideas are worth a dime a dozen. What makes the difference is follow-through. Once an idea hits your thinking, you have about ninety seconds to act on it before your brain starts shouting excuses at you. Make a commitment right now to act on your next idea within ninety seconds of coming up with it. Put your idea into motion. A simple action creates commotion and momentum.

Bringing It Home

1. Have you recently given your church a serious checkup? If so, what did you discover? If not, could you do so in the next three months?

2. What has been your church's track record of adopting or adapting popular programs or ministries from other churches? Has it been positive or negative? Why?

3. If you were starting your church all over again today, which ministries would you keep doing? Which ones would you not do? Could you stop doing those ministries today? Why or why not?

4. Where are your present church ministries focused? Are they on evangelism, assimilation, or education? How would you prefer your ministry programs be distributed among these three areas?

10

Equip for Change

Progress is impossible without change, and those who cannot change their minds cannot change anything.

GEORGE BERNARD SHAW

The scene is a familiar one. New generations in the church demand new approaches to worship. A new ministry is started, while another is stopped. A church changes its name in the hope of better communicating with the nonchurched people in the community. A new pastor comes from a different state with a very different culture. In other words, change is in the wind.

Change takes place when something is started or stopped. It is brought about through a logical, step-by-step plan to reach a final goal. Change is regularly delayed, sometimes even stopped, by forces working against it.

129

In trying to move directly from an old situation to a new one, church leaders miss the fact that transition is also taking place. Transition is different from change. It is the process of inner reorientation that people go through as they react to the changes being made in the church. Change only works when transitions work.

To understand what's really happening during change and transition, it is helpful to understand how people adopt a change. Research generally divides people into five types of adopters: innovators, early adopters, middle adopters, late adopters, and laggards[1] (see fig. 10).

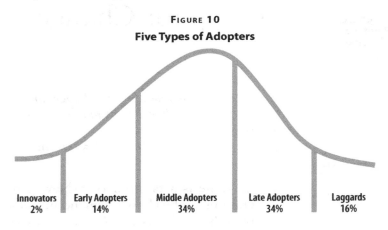

FIGURE 10
Five Types of Adopters

| Innovators 2% | Early Adopters 14% | Middle Adopters 34% | Late Adopters 34% | Laggards 16% |

Five Types of Adopters

In the business world, innovators are called entrepreneurs. In churches, innovators are found in church plants or in churches that vibrantly create new ways of ministry. Innovators regularly talk about the future of the church rather than its past. They love new ideas and relish trying out fresh programs. Since they never saw an innovative idea they didn't like, they quickly latch on to any new vision proposed by church leaders, say, within hours or days of hearing about the vision.

No more than 2 or 3 percent of a church's attendees are innovators, except in new church plants, which may have an unusually large number of them for the first year or two.

Early adopters take a little longer to adopt new approaches for ministry, but they are easily persuaded within one to three months of learning about the changes. They know a good idea when it comes along. Others in the church respect their opinions, allowing them to be highly influential in moving the church forward. Somewhere around 15 percent of church attendees are found in this group.

Middle adopters and late adopters make up the largest portion of worshipers. About 70 percent of a church is found in these two groups, most often evenly divided. Middle adopters react to ideas rather than generating them. They are easily influenced and can go either direction when new ideas are introduced. Late adopters are usually the last people in the church to accept a new idea. They may never verbally acknowledge acceptance of a new direction but will normally go along when the majority of the church approves it. It takes between one and two years to convince late adopters of needed changes but only three to twelve months for middle adopters.

The last group is called laggards, meaning they lag way behind the rest of the church. It requires a great deal of patience and communication to win these people over to changes, and some never adopt the changes. Their unstated motto is "Come weal or woe, we believe in the status quo." Laggards may sow discord after change is accepted or leave if they don't get a hearing or a following.

Making a Transition

When an idea is first introduced to a congregation, there is an initial excitement. As innovators and early adopters quickly buy into the suggested changes, church leaders are lulled to sleep by the apparent lack of resistance. This doesn't last for long, for as soon as the leaders encounter the middle adopters, momentum slows down.

Churches are far better at planning change than they are at planning transition. Leaders begin communicating the needed changes, but after three months a crisis develops, illustrated by the starburst in figure 11. A growing resistance to the anticipated changes creates the crisis.

The resistance is empowered by a lack of transition planning. People can't move into a new day until they let go of the way things used to be and the self-image that supports the old situation. Between the old situation and the new one is a sort of crisis zone where people disengage from the old way of doing church and engage the new way. Change is what takes a church into the crisis zone. Transition is the process of assisting people to move out of the crisis zone, to take the first awkward steps toward the new way of doing things. It is in the crisis zone that the middle and late adopters struggle with their sense of loss. It is here that churches fail in planning how to help people disengage from the old and engage with the new.

FIGURE 11
Crisis Zone

| Innovators 2% | Early Adopters 14% | Middle Adopters 34% | Late Adopters 34% | Laggards 16% |

If church leaders don't plan for transition through the crisis zone, change will most likely fail to materialize or will take a long time to happen. Revitalizing a church requires change *and* transition. In planning for transition, church leaders should first consider if it is worth the work. Completing a transition takes a great deal of time and energy, so be sure you want to do it.

Second, for major changes, leaders should study the transitions that are likely to occur. In other words, who will experience the most disengagement? How many people and who will be affected by the changes? Who is most likely to suffer feelings of loss in the transition? Who will experience the greatest sense of disruption in their ministry and self-esteem? For example, if a church contemplates a change in worship styles, the current worship leaders and musicians are most likely to experience the greatest disengagement and to struggle with transition. For such a change to take place successfully, plans should be made to help these persons deal with a potential sense of loss of identity and their role at the church. They must be helped to find new roles and identities in the church.

Third, church leaders must educate the congregation as to how the changes will affect them. Sharing vision is more than just telling people where the future lies; it also means helping people accept endings. Revitalization leaders understand the natural sense of loss that comes with all changes. Thus, they hold meetings to discuss the endings and encourage others to share their feelings. Church leaders communicate how the church will assist church members in finding new areas of service, ministry roles, and personal identity during the time of transition. Remind people often (1) that there are no unchanging churches, (2) of all the things that will not change, and (3) that change may involve discomfort. Inoculate people against coming changes. If you don't, they will blame you. If you do, the discomfort won't be as bad as you say. If leaders don't take transition planning seriously, the hoped-for changes may never happen.

Fourth, for substantial changes, leaders must plan on communicating them in numerous ways over a two-year period of time. It takes middle adopters and late adopters that long to get on board. Communication must include sermons, announcements, listening meetings, small group discussions, emails, blog discussions, articles in newsletters and on the church website, one-on-one discussions, and any other way of communicating that can be reasonably employed.

Fifth, a team or task force should monitor the communication and process of adoption. The team must listen to what people are saying and be willing to tell the pastor and leaders, "That message didn't get through." Or, "That communication didn't make sense." Or, "The people don't understand." The team also needs to help the pastor and other leaders think through ways to help those most affected by the changes move on with their lives in the new environment.

Most of all, leaders must realize that nothing has happened just because the innovators and early adopters have bought into the proposed changes. That is only the beginning. The hard work is getting acceptance from the middle and late adopters. Communication must continue throughout the crisis zone for successful implementation of new ideas. Effective change agents are those who assist people through the crisis zone. North American pastors and other church leaders tend to run through this zone to get on with a vision. With their sense of busyness, they do not allow time for endings and feelings of loss to take place or for changes to begin properly. Remember, unless your church is in danger of closing, walk slowly through the crisis zone.

CASE STUDY 11
Communicating Change

The board of New Life Church was excited about the new plan for growth. Pastor Johnson eagerly preached a six-part sermon series to cast the initial vision to the congregation. The response of the congregation was positive, and it appeared that nearly 30 percent of the congregation was on board with the new direction for the church.

A year later, though, the plan had ground to a total stop. The excitement that started with the pastor's sermon series was now barely visible.

After a few people raised pointed questions about funding, others started sharing personal fears about the suggested changes. Some shared fears about losing their positions if committees were done away with under the new structure. Others admitted they were fearful that the new changes might fail. Still others just were not convinced the new direction was the best and felt comfortable leaving things alone.

At the last board meeting, the discussion focused on what went wrong. All they could agree on was that what started out with a bang was now just a whimper. Pastor Johnson suggested that perhaps the sermon series had not been enough. He felt that more advertising and communication with the congregation might have helped. Maybe they, the board, had just not communicated well enough.

Analysis:

- What do you think went wrong?
- Did the board understand the difference between change and transition?
- What could they have done differently to ensure greater success?

Change Response Analysis

Conducting a change response analysis is a way to look at the change dynamics of a church. Before beginning such an analysis, consider that there is another way of describing the people who make up a church.

The first group is the radicals. This term is used in some circles in a negative way, but it is used here to refer to people

135

who are an excellent source of new ideas. Most radicals are either innovators or early adopters. They provide a leavening in the church by bringing excitement and energy to bear on the programs and ministry. While not a good source of feedback—they always bring a positive report—they are good at starting new things. One negative is that they burn out quickly. Radicals are not good at finishing what they start. They abound in great numbers in the first decade of a new church but are expelled early when their ideas become too radical for others to support.

A second group is the progressives. This group anticipates growth needs and may see them before the pastor does. They live on the growing edge of the church and like risk and change. Progressives see the benefit of planning and make excellent members of boards and planning teams. They are not only good at spearheading new directions but, unlike the radicals, will also stay to the end. The progressives are the greatest benefit to a revitalization leader because they are able to communicate to the conservatives. They are what the conservatives always wanted to be but couldn't become because of their aversion to risk.

A third group is the conservatives. They typically have the highest credibility of any of the groups but prefer the status quo. Since they are good at saving money, they carry the financial burden of the church. They keep revitalization leaders honest by asking questions that leaders sometimes forget to ask. Conservatives are not risk takers and don't like to jeopardize their personal comfort. They feel pastors exaggerate, and they must be assured of a high level of success before they buy into a project.

A fourth group is the traditionalists. They never buy into change and are dragged along like a caboose on a train. Traditionalists make emotionally reactive statements, but their comments don't slow the church down because progressives and conservatives just ignore them. Radicals react strongly toward traditionalists, and vice versa, since they are both emotional. If too many traditionalists make up a church's attendees, they will resist any and all changes unless they are forced upon them.

Of the four groups of people, the radicals and the progressives are proponents of change, while the conservatives and the traditionalists usually oppose change (see fig. 12).

FIGURE 12
Proponents and Opponents

Proponents   Opponents

| Radicals | Progressives | Conservatives | Traditionalists |

Radicals and progressives are found in large numbers in new church plants. They enjoy taking risks and are attracted to visionary leaders. New churches consist of around 40 percent radicals, 50 percent progressives, and just 5 percent each of conservatives and traditionalists (see fig. 13).

FIGURE 13
First Generation Church

| Radicals 40% | Progressives 50% | Conservatives 5% | Traditionalists 5% |

By the second generation, a church has expelled nearly all of its radicals. Churches that are over twenty years old find it increasingly difficult to begin new ministries in part because radicals now compose only 5 percent or less of the total church. The largest increase is among the conservatives, who represent close to 40 percent of the church. Progressives are reduced to 40 percent, and traditionalists begin to show signs of increasing influence, making up 15 percent of the congregation (see fig. 14).

FIGURE 14

Second Generation Church

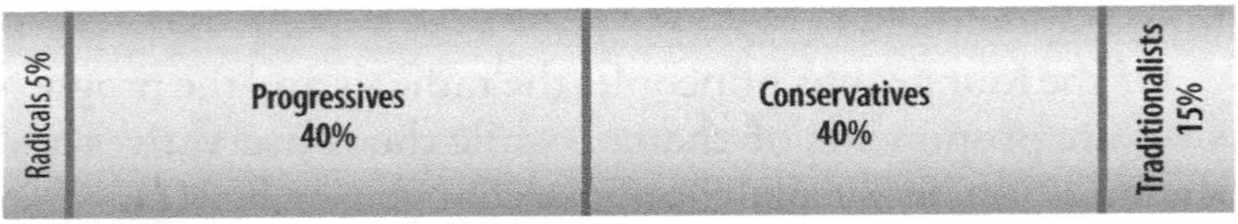

Radicals 5%	Progressives 40%	Conservatives 40%	Traditionalists 15%

By the time a church reaches its third generation, about its fortieth year of existence, the radicals are completely gone. Only 10 percent of the people are found among the progressives. By this time, conservatives and traditionalists each comprise about 45 percent of the congregation (see fig. 15).

FIGURE 15

Third Generation Church

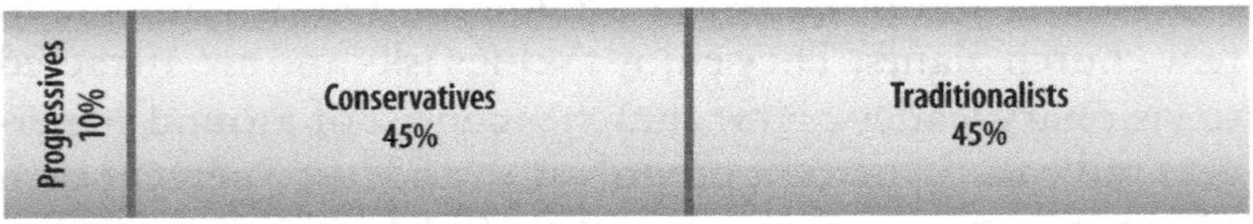

Progressives 10%	Conservatives 45%	Traditionalists 45%

As can be seen from these figures, a positive response to change is most probable in the first or second generation of a church's life cycle. As churches age, they naturally expel the people who are most open to change—radicals and progressives. Over the years, the conservatives and traditionalists gain authority and, with their normal reluctance to take risks, find it difficult to adopt new changes to the church's ministry.

To conduct a change response analysis, a pastor and other church leaders should place all adult attendees into one of the four groups—radicals, progressives, conservatives, and traditionalists. Then they should determine the percentage of each group and develop a chart like those above. In this way, leaders will visually see the challenges ahead. In smaller churches this is done quite easily since most people are well-known by church leaders. Pastors and church leaders can

138

make personal assessments of which categories church attendees fit into. An educated guess is good enough to make a basic analysis.

By conducting a change response analysis, a revitalization leader is able to determine the likelihood that a new direction for the church will be adopted. The more radicals and progressives in a church, the greater the potential for a new vision to be embraced. Of course, the more conservatives and traditionalists in a congregation, the less likely that changes will be adopted.

CASE STUDY 12
Change Response Analysis

Pastor Dugan gazed out his office window, then back at a piece of paper on his desk. He had just drawn a change response analysis chart of his congregation. The drawing looked like the following:

Progressives 5%	Conservatives 45%	Traditionalists 50%

Based on what he knew about progressives, conservatives, and traditionalists, his church on Lookout Mountain was in trouble. He immediately knew from the chart that change was going to be difficult. However, he determined that instead of being discouraged, he would see this as a challenge. As he looked out the window of his small study, he thought of a plan to communicate a new vision for the revitalization of Lookout Mountain Church.

His first thought was to preach a series of sermons on the need for change and a plan for renewal of the church's ministry. Yet, the more he thought about it, the more he felt uneasy with that approach. He had known other pastors who tried preaching a state of the church address, but in every case it

139

had failed to bring about the desired results. Then a different idea popped into his mind, an idea that would take a bit longer but one that might garner greater acceptance by the conservatives and traditionalists.

Pastor Dugan decided that he and his wife would visit all members—singles, couples, and families—to share his vision. Yes, it would take nearly a year to talk with everyone, but using this approach would give everyone personal attention. All would have the opportunity to hear directly from him and to ask questions.

Yes, he thought. *This is the right way to go.*

Analysis:

- Knowing what you know about the four groups of people in a church—radicals, progressives, conservatives, and traditionalists—what challenges are in store for Pastor Dugan?
- Do you think his plan will work? Is there a better way?
- What would you do if you were in his situation?

Bringing It Home

1. How does your church handle change? Have you or your church experienced the crisis zone when moving toward change?

2. Do your leaders understand the difference between change and transition? How could you train your leaders to become aware of both and to manage the transition side of change?

3. What are the percentages of radicals, progressives, conservatives, and traditionalists in your church? What does this tell you about the challenge of change management in your church?

4. What ideas and insights did you gain from this chapter to help you better manage change and transition in your church?

Deal with Resistance

The one who complains about the way the ball bounces is likely the one who dropped it.

LOU HOLTZ

There is no progress without change and transition, and conflict results from both. In truth, it is not changes that cause resistance to a church moving in a new direction but rather the sense of loss experienced in the process. To revitalize any organization, something must be changed and something will be lost.

Take an inventory of the losses current worshipers will suffer. Watch for five kinds of losses:

1. *Loss of identity*. People identify with the roles, positions, or places they occupy in a church. When these are changed, people sense a loss of identity, and some fight to retain it at all costs. Try to identify who

141

will lose their identity, and see if you can place them in a new position where the resulting sense of loss will be mitigated.

2. *Loss of control.* People feel secure when they are in charge. When authority patterns are reconfigured during a time of revitalization, people become fearful. They make statements like, "I didn't ask for this." They ask questions like, "What will they do next?" Give worshipers a sense of control by listening to their concerns and answering their questions.

3. *Loss of meaning.* People find personal meaning in places, programs, and patterns of life. Revitalization actions, such as relocation, removing old furniture, remodeling rooms, and other activities, result in a loss of meaning for some. They ask, "Why is this happening to me?" and say, "I've attended this church for over twenty years. Doesn't that count for anything?" Do everything possible to reassign old meanings to the new. For example, if relocating the church is necessary, take some item of meaning from the old church and place it prominently in the new.

> *Human beings cannot move into new roles with a clear sense of purpose and energy unless they let go of the way things were and the self-image that fit that situation.*
>
> WILLIAM BRIDGES

4. *Loss of belonging.* People desire to see newcomers frequenting worship services but sense loss when overwhelmed by numbers of people they do not know. They say, "I don't even know the people sitting next to me in worship anymore." Give worshipers permission to know only a few people (research has shown that most church members know only about sixty people by first name). Teach the importance of knowing a few well, such as small group members, and demonstrate that acquaintance with all church attendees is not necessary.

5. *Loss of a future.* People hope for a stable future and struggle with the idea that it is changing. They say, "I worked hard to become a board member. Now it seems I'm going to be pushed out." Others comment, "We're not visiting the elderly any longer. I hope the pastor doesn't forget me when I'm in a nursing home." Organize ways to care for people. Let everyone know that people are more important than programs.

The people attending plateaued and declining churches normally sense a need for change in their church. They recognize that things are not right, which may lead to their willingness to back the pastor in a turnaround project. Unfortunately, if feelings of loss are too great, they can lead to increased resistance rather than revitalization.

CASE STUDY 13
Change Creates Loss

Change was needed at Prince of Peace Church. Everyone agreed something had to be done or the church would surely continue its slow demise. Even now attendance was getting to the point of embarrassment. One week less than 30 percent of the seating was occupied, and the one visitor who came looked awkwardly out of place. There were more than enough places to sit, but the guest appeared to flounder as he struggled to decide if he should sit by himself or with the people who were gathered down front.

Prince of Peace was urgently in need of a transition from an old worship style, which used a piano and organ, to one that employed electric guitars and drums. Discussions had gone on for years about this issue, but little was ever done. Younger families continued to drop out, with most attending the new church five blocks away that used a new style of music. The issue was a substantial one, involving a change in the church's philosophy of ministry, a change in worship personnel, and a change in longtime worship practices.

143

Finally, out of deep frustration, Pastor Sands and the board made a decision and implemented it quickly. Meeting with Mary and Sue, who had faithfully played the organ and piano for the past eleven years, Pastor Sands told them directly, "We are changing things. Next Sunday will be your last Sunday to play." Both ladies left the meeting in absolute shock. They had had no advanced warning. As they discussed the situation, they wondered aloud what this change meant for them and their role in the church's future.

Even after two years, Mary and Sue are still reeling from the sudden change. It is not the change in worship style that bothers them. They both enjoy the new music. It is the loss of their identity. Both feel they were tossed aside with no thanks and are no longer valued. Neither has found a new place to serve in the church.

Analysis:

- What is the main issue with Mary and Sue?
- How might Pastor Sands have handled the transition in a better way?
- How has your church dealt with resistance created by ministry changes?

Anticipate Obstacles

A crisis that hits one church may be met with an absence of vision and a complete failure to move in a new direction. In contrast, a similar crisis at another church may be met with an enthusiastic acceptance of a new vision and way of doing things. What makes the difference? One answer, perhaps the main one, is that revitalization leaders anticipate that resistance will occur at some point in the process of changing a church. One researcher points out that the primary reason pastors and other church leaders often settle for plateau and decline in their church is the fear of conflict.[1]

144

A clever revitalization leader prepares to manage resistance and conflict.

Some of the obstacles that rise up to create resistance are called "sacred cows." A sacred cow is a program, ministry, or expectation that people hope to see repeated . . . forever. Revitalization leaders need to be aware of five common sacred cows:

1. *Unwritten cows*: expectations that are not written down in any document, making it likely that a leader will get into trouble when he or she unknowingly encounters it. For example, that so-and-so always directs the vacation Bible school.
2. *Written cows*: expectations or guidelines that are written into church documents. For example, only church members may use the sanctuary for weddings.
3. *Turf cows*: the reality that certain people have rights of usage or oversight of certain programs or facilities. For example, the church secretary has the only key to the church office. It is her turf, and no one else may use the copy machine, or anything else in the office, without her approval.
4. *Denominational cows*: expectations or guidelines from the denomination. For example, only denominational education materials are to be used in the church.
5. *Personal cows*: individual expectations of people attending the church. For example, the pastor should visit members, be available to anyone wishing counseling, pray at every church function, or a host of other expectations. There are almost as many personal cows as there are church attendees, which makes it difficult for pastors to carry on ministry in a pleasing manner.

Revitalization leaders try to identify and address as many of the sacred cows as possible, but they are ready for new cows to appear at any moment.

Another set of obstacles appears in the form of saboteurs. These are people who take a negative bent toward almost every new approach or idea for ministry. Be ready for

- *naysayers*: people who say it'll never work
- *church historians*: people who remember when the church tried it before and that it didn't work then and most likely won't now
- *wait-and-see-ers*: people who want more time to analyze and study the proposed idea, usually to the point of exhaustion
- *old dogs*: people who say "you can't teach an old dog new tricks," thereby refusing to try the new way
- *yeah-buts*: people who always have an excuse or reason for rejecting a new idea

Know who these people are in your church and be prepared with an answer for each one. Whenever you are going to present a new idea, think through what each of the saboteurs is likely to say or ask. Prepare your answers ahead of time. Don't let yourself be caught off guard.

Conduct a For/Against Analysis

Take a piece of paper and write the name of your revitalization project or idea at the top of the page. For example, if you are seeking to relocate the church to another part of the city, write RELOCATION at the top of the page.

Then draw a line under the name and separate the page into two halves by drawing another line down the middle of the page. On the left side of the page list all the factors that are providing a push *for* the project, while on the other side of the page list all the factors that are pushing *against* the project (see fig. 16).

Once you have filled out both halves, you can evaluate the probability of the idea being accepted. If you find more

FIGURE 16

Relocation

Factors For		Factors Against	
1.		1.	
2.		2.	
3.		3.	
4.		4.	
5.		5.	
Etc.		Etc.	

factors in the against column, you have two options. Option number one is to try to overpower the factors (people or issues) that oppose your idea. This is the option regularly selected by church leaders, and it rarely yields positive results. Anger, frustration, and church splits are the normal results of power plays in a church.

A better option is to try to remove the factors against the project. For example, if you find that a lack of finances is one of the factors holding the project back, then find a way to raise the money. Once the money is in hand, that factor will be removed from the against column. Or if you find that a particular person is speaking against the project, meet with that person to share your vision, answer questions, and gain support. The more you work to remove the forces against you, the more likely your project will move forward without unneeded conflict and rancor.

Manage Conflict and Criticism

The summer after my junior year of high school I worked for a small lumber company in my hometown. My job, along with three other high school friends, was to unload raw lumber from boxcars that were moved onto the property each evening. Much of the time we had to handle the lumber with our bare hands. Each night, after arriving home, I used tweezers to pull small splinters from the palms of my hands. These small pieces of lumber were irritating, but having them in my hands never stopped me from working.

One day the yard manager put me to work building a wood display to hold some grass seed. In my enthusiasm to do something other than move lumber all day, I accidentally hit my left thumb while hammering nails into the display. In excruciating pain, I dropped the hammer, squeezed my left thumb tightly with my right hand, and muttered some words that a Christian should not say. Regaining my composure, I discovered that I could not continue working. My thumb was so swollen that I couldn't grasp or hold anything with my left hand. The result? I did not work for the rest of the week.

This story illustrates the difference between criticism and conflict. Criticism is similar to the small splinters of wood that I got in my hands each day. Splinters, and criticism, are irritating but will not stop you from working. Hitting my thumb is similar to conflict. It creates so much pain that you have to stop working and deal with the issue.

Criticism is critique that causes minor frustrations. All pastors and church leaders are critiqued. Leaders always suffer the pain of public and private evaluation of their ideas and actions. Conflict is that point in the critique where the frustration is so great that you have to stop what you are doing and deal with the issues before moving on. Conflict literally means to strike together, and that's exactly what I did when I hit my thumb with the hammer. The result was that I had to stop working and deal with the pain. When the pain of critique becomes so great that you can no longer do ministry, you have reached a point

> *Leaders will be scrutinized, idolized, and criticized. Scrutinized because our work is done in public. Idolized because our work is done on a pedestal. Criticized because our work is done with people.*
>
> J. GRANT HOWARD

of conflict. Something must be done or the ministry will not continue.

Types of Conflict

All conflict is not the same. There are at least three predominant types:

1. Substantive conflict is conflict over issues. It focuses on facts, methods, values, and ideas.
2. Interpersonal conflict is conflict between people. It focuses on feelings, attitudes, and personal understandings.
3. Intrapersonal conflict is conflict within oneself. It focuses on inner feelings, beliefs, and self-esteem.

Eighty percent of church conflicts are over substantive issues. For example, whether the offering should be taken at the end of the worship service or after the second hymn is a procedural issue. Such matters are not clearly articulated in the Bible and thus are a matter of practice or custom, yet they create heated disagreements in churches. Substantive conflict can also generate interpersonal and intrapersonal conflicts. In numerous churches, the substantive issue is not as important as people make it out to be at the time. Years later people forget the issue and remember the interpersonal conflict.

Steps for Managing Conflict

True conflict is rarely solved, but in most situations it can be managed so that it doesn't injure the church or stall the efforts toward revitalization. The process is usually messy and never a simple 1-2-3 process. Yet, it may be helpful to think of the process in a step-by-step manner in order to get a clear picture of what to do.

First, identify when criticism actually becomes conflict. As you initiate changes, transitions, and new procedures, you will be criticized. Remember, criticism is not conflict. It only becomes conflict when the pain it causes reaches the point where ministry can't continue until something is done about it.

Second, identify the type of conflict. Is it substantive, interpersonal, or intrapersonal? If it is substantive, what is the issue? Focus on the issue and try not to engage inter- or intrapersonal feelings. If the conflict is interpersonal, ask those involved to meet together to see if they can make amends and reach an acceptable agreement. If it's intrapersonal, talk to God about it in your prayers, asking for the grace to change yourself or to forgive others.

Third, identify the norms of the situation. Norms are the normal way things are done at your church. What is an acceptable way of dealing with conflict issues? The wisest approach is to work within your norms as much as possible.

Fourth, identify the rules of the situation. Investigate your constitution, bylaws, denominational book of order, and any policy guidelines that may be in place. Also consider if there are unwritten policies that are usually followed. Be sure to follow whatever written rules are available when managing conflict.

Fifth, identify the contingencies. What is the price you or your family will have to pay in the management of the conflict? What will you lose? What will you stand to gain? Is it worth it? Remember, all battles are not worth fighting. Choose carefully which battles you fight.

Sixth, identify the potential actions of others. What have you seen others do previously? What are they likely to do now? Know people well enough to predict their actions and be prepared for them.

Seventh, identify the values of the situation. What ought to be done? What is right? What is biblical? At all times seek to manage conflict within the guidelines of Scripture.

150

Eighth, identify the assumptions of the situation. What foundational beliefs are involved? What is believed to be true? What is expected? What is traditional? Knowing the assumptions that undergird people's understandings will provide great insight into how to manage a situation.

At this point, having thought about the eight steps, pause. Take time to think about the proper approach and what action to take. What results do you want to see? What is the best way to approach the situation? There are at least five ways to approach any conflict. Each approach is appropriate depending on the situation and the results you desire to achieve.

Option 1: surrender the project in order to keep relationships intact.

If you feel that relationships with the persons involved in the conflict are more important than the project itself, you may find it best to put the plan off for a time in order to remain in good standing. The key question: Is it worth fighting about?

Option 2: give up the relationships to win the battle.

In some cases, you may sense that your side of the issue must be pressed to a winning conclusion. While every battle is not worth fighting, some are. The bottom line is that the cost will be high. People will say things that are hurtful, and your family may bear the brunt of the overall distasteful result. Perhaps people will leave the church. The key question: Are you willing to pay the price?

Option 3: ignore the conflict altogether.

If the conflict is between a few people, it often is best to ignore it. Pastors and church leaders are not required to solve every conflict that arises in the church, particularly between adults. Only if the conflict affects the entire church must those leaders get involved. The key question: Is the conflict creating significant problems for the entire church?

Option 4: obtain concessions from those on both sides of the issue.

Obtaining concessions involves compromise. Seek to negotiate concessions from those on each side of the issue until an agreement is reached that allows you to move forward on the idea, even if it is only a small move forward. The conflict may not be settled, but at least you can move forward. The key question: Can we work together to move forward?

Option 5: create a win for all parties involved in the conflict.

If this can be accomplished, the effect is greater than the whole. For example, when a church decides to have two worship services using two different styles, both parties win by getting to worship entirely in their preferred style, but the overall church wins too. The key question: Is there a way for each party to win?

Dealing with resistance is a major skill that revitalization leaders must learn and employ. The goal is not to eliminate criticism or conflict but to manage them so they don't sap the energy of the congregation. Honest peace is not found in the absence of criticism or conflict but in the presence of creative responses that lead people into the future with grace.

CASE STUDY 14
Managing Conflict

It was time. Things around South Bend Church had gone on long enough. At first the criticism was bearable, but now it had reached a point where the issue had to be settled before the church could move forward in unity.

The issue? Two years ago Pastor Silvers and the board had introduced the idea of selling the church facility and relocating to the west side of town to start over. All the new growth in the city was on the west side of town. After going through an extensive evaluation by a well-known consultant, it was determined that relocation was the number one way to revitalize the church.

The Millers and the Thompsons, both longtime members of South Bend, stood staunchly against such a move. At the first congregational meeting to discuss the idea, Mike Miller, the patriarch of his large family, walked to the front of the room in full view of everyone and, placing his hands on the bricks in the front wall, said, "Pastor, I can't leave. See these bricks? I put them into this wall with my own hands. I can't bear the thought of leaving."

After Mr. Miller returned to his seat, Mrs. Thompson stood and addressed the meeting. Her concern was the fact that her brother, now deceased, had painted the mural of Jesus's baptism on the wall above the baptistry. "If we move," she asked, "what will happen to my brother's painting?"

Discussion of a potential relocation went downhill from then on. The Millers' and the Thompsons' criticisms of the idea of relocating South Bend Church turned sour. When they started attacking Pastor Silvers's wife and children, it was enough. Pastor Silvers decided it was time to challenge them. If the church was going to have any chance of thriving in the future, they had to be removed from leadership.

Analysis:

- What type of conflict is South Bend Church experiencing?
- What leadership approach has Pastor Silvers decided to employ?
- What questions would you want to ask and answer before you took the same approach?

Bringing It Home

1. What losses are people in your church likely to experience if the church goes through a process of revitalization? How can you work to minimize the resistance their feelings will generate?

2. Which of the sacred cows and saboteurs have you encountered? Which ones are most likely to appear during the process of revitalization?

3. Select one change you would like to see happen in your church and list factors for and against it. Brainstorm ways to remove the obstacles that stand against the change and begin to put the ideas into practice.

4. How has conflict been managed in your church's past? What can you do this month to begin training your people to deal with conflict in a more appropriate manner?

12

Stay the Course

Church Revitalization Chart

See the Potential

Commit to Lead

Assess the Situation

Learn the Principles

Discern God's Vision

Build a Coalition

Lift the Morale

Make Hard Decisions

Refocus the Ministry

Equip for Change

Deal with Resistance

Stay the Course

Breaking Through

Life is like riding a bicycle—to keep your balance you must keep moving.

ALBERT EINSTEIN

Pastors commonly use stories in their sermons to illustrate various points. A favorite story among pastors reportedly originated with a lecture given by Winston Churchill on October 29, 1941, when he visited Harrow School. Various versions of the story have been passed around from pastor to pastor, but my guess is that nearly every pastor has used some version of the story at least one or more times.

What is the story? One version says that Prime Minister Churchill stood before the students and said, "Never, ever, ever, ever, ever, ever, ever give in. Never give in. Never give in. Never give in." After which he said no more and just

155

sat down, making, so the myth goes, such a strong impact on the students that they never forgot the speech.

It's a good story, and there is no doubt the students never forgot the speech. However, Churchill gave a slightly longer speech and used slightly different words than normally quoted. The speech came after he had gained hope that Britain could survive and even win the war. In the first years of World War II, Britain had stood almost alone against Nazi Germany. The future looked bleak until March and June of 1941. In March, Churchill learned that the United States was going to furnish Britain with war supplies. In June, Germany invaded the Soviet Union, which deflected some of the Nazi war effort away from Britain. Thus, by the time of the Harrow School speech, he had a growing hope that the outcome of the war could be positive for Britain.

When he stood to address the students at Harrow School, his optimism came through. He said, "Never give in. Never give in. Never, never, never, never—in nothing, great or small, large or petty—never give in, except to convictions of honor and good sense. Never yield to force. Never yield to the apparently overwhelming might of the enemy."[1]

Yes, the story is a bit different from that commonly heard in sermons, but the point is the same. Churchill told the students never to give in, and his words were supported by his fresh optimism, his growing sense of hope.

Do you have a sense of optimism for your church? Do you believe there is hope for your church? If so, then take Churchill's advice and never give in.

As you realize by this point of the book, bringing revitalization to a church is difficult work. Resources are often slim, opposition is often strong, and victories are often small. It's tempting to give up—usually too soon.

In part, a desire to give up comes from a misunderstanding of what it takes to be successful. Two stories, both from the world of sports, have helped me hang in there, even in tough times.

Lessons from Leaders

Like many people, perhaps even you, I've been a fan of legendary basketball coach John Wooden for years. He coached the UCLA basketball team to ten national championships, seven of them in a row! Wooden was one of the most successful basketball coaches in history, and his records are not likely to be broken any time soon.

The tendency is to see only his victories, which took place in the last twelve years of his coaching career. Before winning the national championships for which he is so well known, Wooden struggled in his coaching career. Describing those years of struggle, and how they related to his eventual success, Wooden commented:

> Yet, to truly understand how the record was accomplished, it is important to realize that I coached for more than twenty-five years before my first NCAA Championship team was crowned. Our ultimate success came from following a philosophy that allowed us to feel successful all during those years of struggle before the first championship banner was raised.
>
> We held firm to the belief that success is not determined by the scoreboard, or even by the won/lost record. Instead, we saw success as an internal feeling resulting from the self-satisfaction of knowing we'd given our best to become the best of which we were capable.[2]

For almost two-thirds of his twenty-seven-year career at UCLA, John Wooden coached without winning a championship. He was hired in 1948, and it was 1964 before his basketball team won the first of an eventual ten NCAA championships. What if he had given up in the first sixteen years? It's an interesting question. If he had left in 1963, there would have been no NCAA championships. The four undefeated seasons of 30-0 would not have materialized. The men's all-time winning streak of eighty-eight games over four seasons

157

would never have happened. But Wooden did stay, and, as is commonly said, "The rest is history."

The story of professional baseball player Pat Tabler is less well known than that of John Wooden. Tabler played professional baseball for seventeen years, seven in the minor league and ten in the major league. Over his career, he was selected for one all-star game and played in one world series. A look at his batting average and career earnings is revealing (see fig. 17).[3]

FIGURE 17
Pat Tabler's Salary and Batting Average

Minor Leagues	Salary	Batting Average
1976	$2,500	.231
1977	$3,000	.238
1978	$3,500	.273
1979	$4,750	.316
1980	$5,000	.296
1981	$15,000	.301
1982	$25,000	.342
Major Leagues		
1983	$51,000	.291
1984	$102,000	.290
1985	$275,000	.275
1986	$470,000	.326
1987	$605,000	.307
1988	$800,000	.282
1989	$825,000	.259
1990	$725,000	.273
1991	$800,000	.216
1992	$800,000	.252
Total	$5,511,750	.280

Note how the early years of Tabler's career didn't appear to be fantastic, especially his salary. He labored along in the minor league with no guarantee that he'd be called up to the majors. Since his batting average gradually improved, he did have hope, but no guarantee. He may have thought of quitting and finding a better-paying job. Yet, he hung in there and later reaped large rewards.

What would have happened if he had quit in the first seven years? He would not have played in the all-star game or the world series. And he would not have reached the high level of income he did. But he persevered and ended up with a successful seventeen-year career.

The moral of these stories is clear: stay the course. Although he wasn't thinking about church revitalization, Ross Perot, a former US presidential candidate, declared, "Most people give up when they're about to achieve success. They quit on the one-yard line. They give up at the last minute of the game, one foot from a winning touchdown."[4] Once you've started down the path to revitalization, stay the course. It's always too soon to quit.

The Fox and the Hedgehog

One of the most talked about concepts in the last few years involves a fox and a hedgehog. The story comes from ancient Greek literature and was summarized in an aphorism by Greek philosopher Archilochus. It simply states, "The fox knows many things, but the hedgehog knows one big thing."[5]

Foxes tend to move around quickly, chasing new ideas. They find it difficult to stay with one vision or direction for very long, preferring to jump from one idea to another. Hedgehogs are quite the opposite. They tend to move much slower but find it easy to stay with one vision or one direction until it is accomplished.

Pastors can be foxes or hedgehogs. If they are foxes, they may not have the patience or tenacity to stay long enough to see revitalization take place. Revitalization leaders are hedgehogs to one degree or another. They keep moving forward until revitalization happens. In short, they stay the course and never give up.

Former prime minister Winston Churchill said, "Success is not fatal, failure is not final; it is the courage to continue that counts." God said it more clearly: "Therefore, my beloved brethren, be steadfast, unmovable, always abounding in the work of the Lord, knowing that your toil is not in vain in the Lord" (1 Cor. 15:58).

Case Study 15
Staying the Course

Calvary Church was started in 1956 by Pastor Paul Minters. At twenty-five years old, Pastor Minters looked to the future with passion and vision. A strong authoritarian leader, he directed the church with a firm hand, leading to sixteen straight years of growth. During those years, the church purchased five acres of land and built a 500-seat sanctuary, a large education building, and a fellowship hall. His success caught the eyes of the other pastors in his state, and he was elected as the general director of his denomination. The congregation of Calvary voted to name the education building after him and placed a plaque over the entrance that read PAUL MINTERS BUILDING.

Upon his departure, the church was averaging 1,300 in worship attendance.

The next eight years were nothing short of disastrous as three pastors came and went in quick succession. The first pastor came from a church of only 210 members and soon found he was a mismatch with the larger Calvary Church. The second pastor was a passive leader who did not have the directive style of Pastor Minters. The third pastor came from a well-known megachurch, but the philosophy of ministry he tried to implement received a cool reception from the congregation at Calvary, and he soon left in disgust. By the time he left, the church was averaging only 275 attendees and had suffered

160

eight years of decline—18 percent per year or nearly 85 percent for the eight years.

Jim Peters accepted the call of Calvary Church to be their fifth pastor. Even though he knew Calvary was in need of revitalization, he decided there was no desperation. Instead of trying to change things quickly, he determined to move slowly but deliberately to refocus Calvary outwardly. Gradually, he made small changes that in time added up to big change. He took his time in building a new coalition and, as opportunity presented itself, guided new people onto the church's board of directors. He often told others that his philosophy was to lead people rather than prod them.

The church now averages 525 worshipers and just started a third worship service on Saturday evening. Under Pastor Peters's slow but sure direction, the church is involved in doing mission more than just supporting missions. He has made shifts from a music leader to a worship leader, from organ music to electronic music, from an authoritarian leadership style to a collegial leadership style, from an inward focus to an outward focus.

Morale is high at Calvary Church, and most of the worshipers feel the best days of the church are still in the future. No one appears to remember much about the difficult days when the church declined so rapidly. Of course, people warmly remember Pastor Paul Minters. His name is still over the entrance to the education building, but Pastor Peters doesn't mind.

Analysis:

- Is Pastor Jim Peters a fox or a hedgehog? How do you know?
- What challenges did Pastor Peters face upon coming to Calvary Church?
- How did Pastor Peters approach the challenges?

Bringing It Home

1. Are you a hedgehog or a fox? Give an illustration from your past that illustrates one or the other.

2. Have you ever felt like quitting? If so, did you end up staying or quitting? Did you make the right decision? How do you know?

3. Do you know of anyone who left a job, career, or ministry too soon?

4. Are you committed to staying the course in your ministry? Or do you think it is time to leave? Explain your reasoning.

Breaking Through

We are what we repeatedly do. Excellence then, is not an act, but a habit.

ARISTOTLE

Ten years from now, will your church be thriving or surviving? Will it even be in existence? As it turns out, what happens is largely a matter of making conscious choices today. Success is not about having the coolest pastor or the most creative programs or even being in the best location, although those things might be helpful. Thriving is about making decisions and staying with your choices until they succeed. It's about making progress along the church revitalization chart, taking the necessary risk to engage future potential.

Where Are You on the Church Revitalization Chart?

As you progress along the steps of the church revitalization chart, you will go through four stages: investigation, development, introduction, and implementation (see fig. 18).

163

FIGURE 18

Stages in Church Revitalization

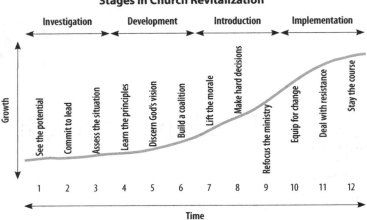

Revitalization begins as you see the potential, commit to lead, and assess the situation of your church. Upward progress is slow at this point but gradually gains momentum as you move into the second stage: development.

A body at rest tends to remain at rest unless some force acts upon it. The discernment of a vision and the creation of a coalition begin to act upon the church body to push it forward. As you learn the principles of revitalization, discern God's vision, and start to build a willing coalition of like-minded people, development begins to materialize.

When you introduce a positive attitude about the future and people regain a renewed sense of pride in the church, others will take notice. Seeing you make the hard decisions alerts everyone to the fact that it is a new day in the life of the church. Refocusing the ministry on those outside the church signals that the church is on the move in a new direction.

Any movement creates friction, which produces heat . . . and conflict. Thus, as you implement a fresh vision, along with new ministries and programs, resistance is sure to rise up to block the new growth. Equipping leaders to understand the impact of change, deal with any resistance, and stay the course allows growth to continue.

Go back to figure 18 and place an X on the curved line to show where you are in the process of revitalization. If you have trouble figuring out where you are, answer the following questions.

Directions: Check the box under the word that best answers each question.

	Yes	Unsure	No
1. Are you hopeful about your church's future?	☐	☐	☐
2. Are you committed to lead the church toward revitalization?	☐	☐	☐
3. Have you assessed the church's situation so that you understand the obstacles and challenges it faces?	☐	☐	☐
4. Have you studied the principles and practices of revitalization?	☐	☐	☐
5. Have you discerned God's vision and communicated it to worshipers one-on-one?	☐	☐	☐
6. Have you built a new coalition of people to assist in the revitalization process?	☐	☐	☐
7. Are you working to lift the morale and attitudes of the congregation?	☐	☐	☐
8. Have you made the hard decisions that are needed to revitalize the church?	☐	☐	☐
9. Have you refocused the church's ministry on evangelism and outreach?	☐	☐	☐
10. Have you equipped leaders to understand and embrace change?	☐	☐	☐
11. Have you trained leaders on how to deal with resistance to change?	☐	☐	☐
12. Are you staying the course and not giving in to pressure to return to the status quo?	☐	☐	☐
Total of each column	—	—	—

Key: 1–3 yes answers = investigation stage
    4–6 yes answers = development stage
    7–9 yes answers = introduction stage
    10–12 yes answers = implementation stage

If you are . . .

- *in the investigation stage*: obtain a church health checkup. The classic definition of a consultant is a man or woman who borrows your watch and charges you a fee to tell you the time. You can do your own investigation, and you should, but some churches look at their watch and can't tell the time. If your church finds it impossible to see things clearly, consider hiring an outside consultant to give you a complete analysis of the church's obstacles and potentials. Doing so will assist you in determining the future of the church and your own level of commitment.

- *in the development stage*: read four to five books from the reading list found in appendix C and make a list of insights and ideas for bringing new life to a church. Create dissatisfaction with the status quo. Take church leaders to conferences to see what other vibrant churches are doing, or assign leaders to visit churches that have experienced renewal and make a report to the rest of the board. Consider inviting a fellow pastor who has helped a church renew its vitality to lead a retreat for your leaders.

- *in the introduction stage*: develop a series of breakthrough projects—that is, projects that will succeed and build valuable morale among members of the congregation. Then, after a few early victories, design a pilot program as an experiment to try out a new approach to ministry. If the pilot program succeeds, keep it going. If it doesn't, remind everyone it was only an experiment and pilot a new ministry.

  Be sure to call a lot of plays. When football coaches call plays in a game, each play is designed to score a touchdown, but most don't. The reason? There's an opposition working against them. To gain yardage, coaches call a lot of plays and go with the ones that work. When it comes to developing new ministries, call a lot of plays until you find the ones that work. Some will not work due to opposition, but when you find a ministry that is fruitful, keep using it.

> *Dissatisfaction is a one-word definition for motivation.*
> CHARLES ARN

- *in the implementation stage*: once your church starts making headway toward new health and vitality, put together a strategic plan for the future. Find out WOTS up (Weaknesses, Opportunities, Threats, Strengths) in your church. Assign members of your team to analyze your church's weaknesses, opportunities, threats, and strengths. Then based on your discoveries, put together a two- to five-year plan.

There are two types of churches: problem-based and possibility-based. The leaders of problem-based churches believe that all their problems will be solved when their problems are solved. The leaders of possibility-based churches believe it's possible to grow when they think of possibilities. Is your church problem-based or possibility-based? What do you want it to be? Wherever you are on the church revitalization chart, take action. Start moving forward.

Think or Thwim

Thomas Watson's name is legendary in business circles. When he took over the Computing-Tabulating-Recording Company (CTR) in 1914, the company was ailing. Very few people even remember that company today, but everyone knows IBM, the company Thomas Watson created out of CTR.

One of the problems Watson faced was the low morale of the employees. In an effort to raise morale and change the attitude of the people, he started plastering signs and slogans on stationery and office walls. Some of the most memorable slogans are:

There is no such thing as standing still.

We must never feel satisfied.

We forgive thoughtful mistakes.

The most famous of his slogans was just one word: think. In fact, the monthly information newsletter for the company was called "Think." But this was just the last of five key words he often used: read—listen—discuss—observe—think. Not a bad outline for anyone trying to revitalize a church too.

Read and reread this book and others about church revitalization. Listen to pastors, church consultants, and other trusted advisors to glean insight. Discuss ideas with your church leaders, especially those on your new coalition. Observe what other leaders have done to revitalize their church. Think about what your church must do to experience new life and vitality in the years ahead. Then add two more words: pray and act. Pray for God's guidance and most of all for courage. Then act! Get started on the steps in the church revitalization chart. Nothing will happen unless you begin.

One day someone penned the following words under Thomas Watson's think sign: or thwim. While the person who scrawled the extra words was trying to be funny, there is truth in the saying: think or thwim. When it comes to revitalizing a business, or a church, it's sink or swim. There is no possibility of victory in continuing to sink. It is only by swimming toward the future that a church will be revitalized.

So picture your church in the not-too-distant future. Imagine a gradually changing attitude reflecting a new sense of expectancy. Imagine people with a contagious enthusiasm for Christ and your church. Imagine classes pulsating with new life. Imagine a new spirit of hope in your church.

Is it possible? The answer . . . a resounding yes! It is possible. Indeed, God very much wants to see it happen. Do you believe that? I do. Can you see the possibilities? I can. Just think about it. There's hope for your church!

Appendix A

Rebirthing a Church

A common statement heard among church planters is, "It is easier to give birth than to raise the dead." Such a statement implies that it is wiser to plant new churches than to raise dead or rapidly declining churches to new life. Church planters have a point. When we observe physical life, it is much easier to have a baby than to raise a dead person to life. Giving birth is a natural occurrence of life. Raising the dead takes a unique act of God. Yes, it is easier to give birth than raise the dead. But the dead can be raised! Even dead churches.

Very few concepts stimulate the mind as much as that of new birth. These words remind us of the new life that is received when one puts his or her faith in Christ. The apostle Paul declares, "Or do you not know that all of us who have been baptized into Christ Jesus have been baptized into his death? Therefore we have been buried with Him through baptism into death, so that as Christ was raised from the dead through the glory of the Father, so we too might walk in *newness of life*" (Rom. 6:3–4, emphasis added). We must continually remind ourselves that God is in the restoration business.

The resurrected life of Jesus Christ resides in each and every believer. Since believers make up the church, the new life of Christ resides in every local assembly. In Revelation 2, God speaks to the church in Ephesus about returning to its first love: "Therefore remember from where you have fallen, and repent and do the deeds you did at first" (v. 5). The power to renew itself already resided in the church at Ephesus, as it does in every church in existence today through the resurrection power of Jesus Christ. Throughout the years, church leaders have often spoken of this possibility for church restoration as renewal or revival. One of the new models of church ministry being used today is the rebirth model. Rebirthed churches are those that are restored to new life and vitality through ceasing to use one form of ministry and replacing it with an alternate form of more effective ministry.

Perhaps the most common approach to rebirthing a church takes place as follows. First, an established church recognizes that its present ministry is not working. Indeed, the church may be approaching the end of a slow decline, which has jeopardized the church's financial integrity. Second, a small core of people envision a new future for the church. Third, through a series of events and meetings, the church agrees to close its public ministry and release current members to join other churches or to commit to becoming part of a new direction for the church. Legal status, such as state corporation, is kept active so that the rebirthed church can burst forth with a new public ministry later on. Appropriate legal changes, such as a new church name, are made as needed to the old corporation. Fourth, following a six- to twelve-month cocooning, during which prayer and plans for a new church take place, the church rebirths itself and opens as a new church.

Candidates for Rebirthing

Churches that are candidates for rebirthing have certain characteristics.

They are usually very small. As one might expect, churches that go through a rebirth are usually quite small. Memories of effective ministry in years gone by provide the main source of corporate self-esteem. Larger churches sense no need to go through a rebirth because their ministry continues to reach enough new people to keep the church healthy. Churches with more than two hundred people have enough strength to use the steps mentioned in previous chapters. Churches averaging less than two hundred people in worship will be most open to a rebirth. Even among them, it is usually churches with less than fifty people at the main morning worship service that are serious candidates for a rebirth.

They are generally ineffective in ministry. The smaller a church becomes, the more difficult it is for it to provide any semblance of effective ministry. A lack of attendance causes worship services to feel hollow. A loss of funds due to limited giving units results in less money for outreach. Older congregations may face deteriorating neighborhoods and facilities with no ability to refurbish them to attract a new generation desiring a higher quality of ministry. While these churches do serve some members, they inherently understand that their days are numbered if something doesn't change. However, they may deny the signs of decline for many years before taking action.

They usually have a core group of people who have a vision for a new style of ministry. Amid the declining attendance, deteriorating facilities, and reduced capacity for ministry, a core group of people exists with a vision for renewed growth. The core may be as small as six or seven people, or it may be as large as fifty to seventy-five. It is a fact that for a church to be rebirthed, there must be a core group of people who have the vision and passion to see it take place.

They usually have a senior pastor with a vision for a new style of church, perhaps with a church-planting background. The senior pastor must be a part of the core. Otherwise, for rebirth to take place, a new pastor will need to be called to give leadership and shape to the vision. In many cases, the senior pastor is well versed or experienced in church planting. At the heart of the rebirthed model is the replanting of a church within a church. The same skills that are needed to plant a church are most often called for in rebirthing a church.

They usually have a sense of desperation. Without question, the main driving force behind most rebirthed churches is an overwhelming sense of desperation. Members and leaders in the church realize that something must be done or the church will close its doors. Defining desperation in practical terms is difficult, but the following should be examined to see if a church should consider rebirthing:

1. *Public worship attendance.* A church needs at least fifty adults to have a public worship service that is attractive to new people. An attendance of twenty to forty adults at worship signals an unhealthy situation. An attendance of less than twenty adults is a strong indication the church should be rebirthed.
2. *Total giving units.* It usually takes a minimum of ten to twelve faithful giving units to provide for a full-time pastor. It takes another ten to twelve units to provide for the ministry of a church in terms of supplies, advertising, and basic ministry. A church reaches a danger point when it has twenty-five or fewer giving units.
3. *Lay leadership pool.* As a rule, a church needs one leader for every ten adult members (junior high and up), one leader for every six elementary school children, and one leader for every two children below school age. Fewer leaders than this will make it difficult to provide for the needs of a growing ministry.

4. *An effective ministry.* A church needs at least one ministry for which it is known in the community. For example, some churches may be known as the church with the great Sunday school, others for their children's program.

5. *Past growth rate.* A growth rate that has been declining for five to ten years should serve as a warning sign. If a church is about one-fourth or less of its original size, it is likely facing hard times that may result in closure if rebirthing does not take place.

6. *The congregation's spiritual health.* Is the church characterized as one of peace, happiness, and love? Or is it one of anger, bitterness, and discouragement?

7. *Average membership tenure.* How long have people been attending the church? If the average membership tenure is more than twenty years, it is a sign the church is having difficulty reaching and assimilating new people. In a location with high mobility, an average tenure of over ten years is still too long.

8. *Goals.* Is the focus of the church on itself or outward to new people? Do leaders talk about ministry, mission, and purpose? Or do they talk about paying the bills, hanging on, real estate, the past, and member care?

9. *Budget expenditures.* Where is the money invested? Is it invested in outreach, advertising, and ministry? Or are these areas the first to be cut when the budget is tight?

10. *Church rumors.* Is there positive talk about God and his work in the church? Are there people who believe God can renew the church in the days ahead? Or do people talk about the past, respond pessimistically to visionary statements, and fail to recognize that God is at work in their church?

It is estimated that in the United States between three thousand and four thousand churches close their doors each year. An additional thirty thousand to forty thousand are on the pathway to closure within the next decade if they do not establish a new direction in ministry. These churches should consider the possibility of rebirthing in their current locations as a way to increase their vitality and fulfill the Great Commission.

Strengths of Rebirthed Churches

Some churches that once were small and almost closed but chose instead to go through a rebirth reveal certain strengths.

They have vision. It takes great faith and vision to close the doors on one ministry in the hope of opening up a new one. No one wants to shut down a ministry that has faithfully served God through the years. Yet, there is a great difference between closing forever and closing to reopen. The first is regretful; the second is visionary. The first takes no faith; the second requires faith. The first removes a testimony to God's work; the second creates a more effective testimony.

They serve as an example of God's renewing work. God is in the business of restoring lost men and women. His creative work continues to be demonstrated every time a person receives him as Lord and Savior. In a similar manner, God's power to restore is revealed in a local body of believers pulled back from the edge of desperation to a new ministry.

They make good use of facilities, money, and people. Churches on the brink of closing down are not very good stewards of the resources God has granted them. By redirecting resources that are no longer being used well, rebirthed churches discover more promising ministries and programs that reach new people for Christ. Often this means selling property and relocating to new areas where a church can begin with a fresh vision. It always means the elimination of ineffective programs from yesteryear and the investing of

time, energy, and money into new ways to reach new generations for Christ.

They have a much larger attendance than the previous congregation. Once a church determines to rebirth itself, it gains new energy and focus. As the core leaders dream, strategize, and plan for a new church, new life emerges that attracts new people to the church. The spirit is reminiscent of that of a new church plant. People are drawn to the new church because they want to be on the ground floor of the new enterprise. As a result, often more people attend the rebirthed church than the former one.

They have enthusiasm and flexibility for a new ministry. After years of effective ministry, established churches fall into the trap of keeping ministries even when they are no longer effective. It is nearly impossible to crawl out of such a repetitive rut to create newer forms of ministry capable of reaching new generations of people. Rebirthing a new church out of the ashes of the old one creates the opportunity to attempt new ways to reach out. This new flexibility brings about a fresh enthusiasm for church growth.

Cautions to Be Considered

People who are making the decision to rebirth a church should do so cautiously but in faith, realizing that God is capable of renewing any church that is willing to change. At the same time, they should consider the following cautions.

The church may not reopen. A major issue to be consid-
ered is the fact that once a church closes, it may not reopen due to a number of circumstances. It is possible that the core group will not bond together as well as originally expected. If the core group disintegrates, a stillbirth may result rather than a rebirth.

The rebirth may be a threat to the denomination because of a loss of a church and money. A church that is part of a denominational structure may face criticism for closing its doors even though it plans to reopen. Denominational leaders may voice concern over a lost source of revenue for denominational programs. If a local assembly sells its property, additional concern may be expressed over control of the resulting funds. A church considering rebirth should talk it over at length with denominational leaders, taking care to get their approval and support. In some cases, it is wise to ask for permission in writing and to spell out the length of time the church has to accomplish its rebirthing goal before the denominational leadership steps in to take over.

There may be real estate and building costs. I've found that property and building costs tend to stall the move toward rebirthing a church. This is especially true when an established church feels it should sell its present property and facilities. The fear is that the higher cost of purchasing land and building facilities at today's rates are too expensive for the rebirthed church to overcome. While costs for such items are high in today's economy, such concern should not be an obstacle. The greatest obstacle to growth is a lack of vision. When a church has a vision, it can accomplish much. Many churches are being planted in our expensive economy, and a rebirthed church with renewed vision and energy will be able to accomplish much more than a dying established church.

Money should be managed carefully. Care must be taken to handle all money with integrity, especially when large funds result from the sale of a building or property. In most states, the funds derived from the sale of property and facilities belonging to nonprofit corporations may not accrue to the benefit of a single individual or group of individuals. Thus, church leaders should be extremely diligent to protect such funds in a fiscally responsible manner.

Don't take too long before rebirthing the church. Once a rebirth begins in earnest, it is best if the new church goes public within twelve months. The trick is to go public before you lose the momentum of the core group but not before the church is able to accomplish an effective rebirth.

The rebirthed model is especially helpful for churches that are in desperate situations following several years of decline. Rather than closing their doors of ministry forever, they should seriously consider rebirthing a new form of ministry.

Appendix B

Church Mergers

When churches decline to the point of desperation, invariably the talk turns to possibilities of merging with another church. As a rule, such mergers are fraught with more difficulties than anyone suspects beforehand. You might think, for instance, that two churches could agree on simple issues, such as what the word *worship* means, but this is not necessarily the case.

If you have lived through a merger, you know that they work only if they are well thought out beforehand. The ones that work best are those in which the church leaders at both churches (or three churches) take the time to understand thoroughly what they are getting into. They must be willing to build a new culture that makes use of the best from both churches and be honest with members of both churches about all aspects of the merger. A forced merger, or one that moves too quickly, often leads to poor morale, which makes a weak foundation for a successful church.

Over the last few decades, numerous churches have attempted a merger (no one knows for sure how many have tried this option), and their stories can easily be found on the internet. There are positive stories as well as negative ones. So take an hour and read through the various stories to catch a glimpse of the possibilities and the problems.

The trouble is that very few churches, or businesses for that matter, seem to get mergers right. Studies by McKinsey & Co. show that of businesses that merged over a ten-year period, only 23 percent were able to recover the costs incurred in the deal. The American Management Association examined fifty-four big mergers and found that about half of them did poorly in terms of productivity, costs, or both.[1]

In much the same way, so many church mergers fail to deliver what they promise that there should be a presumption of failure. The burden of proof should be on showing that anything good can come out of one. However, new research conducted by Warren Bird and Jim Tomberlin has found that plateaued and/or declining churches which became a satellite site of a larger, healthier church often do extremely well.[2]

As with marriage, do not rush into a merger. Churches that successfully merge with others usually take great care to go over every detail of their ministries with a magnifying glass.

Generally, nine out of ten mergers involve churches of the same denomination. Churches that appear to be the least interested in merging are those with a high regard for missions, evangelism, outreach, and church growth. Churches that appear to be the most interested in merging are smaller, declining congregations. In general, the larger the congregation, the more disappointing the results when measured in terms of church membership or worship attendance.

Why Do Congregations Merge?

Churches often consider a merger because of external pressures. A church may be facing a decline in membership, attendance, or giving, which forces it to think of merging with another church. The changing landscape of the neighborhood

180

may create needs for relocating, and merging is one way to accomplish this. Other mergers revolve around concepts of efficiency, economy, and function. However, congregations rarely decide to merge because of one reason. Rather, decisions to merge are often based on a combination of the following:

- a desire to make better use of resources
- a declining or changing community
- a desire to demonstrate Christian unity
- a desire for expanded ministry
- to address church needs
- because of geographical proximity
- for denominational unity
- a desire to survive
- a disaster
- to keep a new church plant alive
- a desire to reduce expenses
- an anticipated increase in membership/attendance
- a desire to merge financial assets
- a desire of pastors to specialize
- a shortage of pastors

Why Church Mergers Fail

Nine out of ten mergers typically fail. If numerical increase is expected, most mergers will not prove successful. The math of church mergers is typically $2 + 2 = 3$. For example, if two churches each averaging 100 worshipers merge, the average worship attendance at the end of the first year together is normally around 150. Or when two churches merge and one averages 50 people at worship and the other averages 30 people, one year later the average worship attendance is about 60 people. Why do mergers fail? There are several reasons.

- The merger is motivated by the wrong reasons, and the churches may not be ready for a merger.
- The differences in tradition, values, styles of ministry, corporate culture, priorities, and theological stances are not taken seriously. Since members of each congregation have spent years developing their own cultures, priorities, and values, they will not change overnight.
- There is a conflict over buildings and property.
- People have unrealized expectations.
- One church moves into another church's building.
- The new church sees few financial savings.
- The new church rebuilds the previous model (i.e., people who come together don't know how to lead a church to the next level).
- There is an incompatibility among leaders.
- Disagreements take place over administrative and leadership structuring.
- An us-versus-them mentality develops.

When Church Mergers Work Best

A few churches do find that merging with another church is a way to revitalize both church ministries. For the most part, mergers work best when the following happen:

- The merger is a result of mission rather than the need to survive.
- The churches have a common theology, philosophy of ministry, values, and corporate culture.
- Both congregations sell their buildings and move into a new building.
- A single pastor or a new pastor is called to lead the congregation.

- The merger is motivated by a strong, future-oriented sense of mission and a desire for expanded outreach.
- Three churches, instead of two churches, merge, and none is dominant. Often when two churches merge, one church feels shut out and loses its sense of identity.
- Time is given to developing solid communication about a possible merger and addressing concerns.
- A significant time for courtship is allowed to take place.

Note: Few mergers meet all these criteria.

Keys to a Successful Merger

You have to go slow to go fast. One result of moving slowly is that people begin to trust one another, and trust is a major ingredient of a successful church merger. The likelihood of a church merger succeeding is increased when churches consider and practice the following ideas:

- Involve laypeople in the planning from the very beginning. Laypeople must feel the idea is theirs and is not imposed on them by church leadership. Eventually, those who must live with the decision must make the decision.
- Before merging, do some small ministries together that can be managed easily. Immediately entering into a church-building program can be detrimental because it is very draining.
- Consider merging with a sister church. It is easier to overcome obstacles when both churches come from the same denomination. Differences can produce creativity in the short term but in the long term most often are detrimental.
- Settle all real estate issues before merging. When two churches come together, real estate considerations tend to dominate the agenda for six to seven years. Be sure

to take the time to investigate the issues surrounding all property before merging.

- Provide open communication. In mergers, there is a tendency to hide what is going on. A great amount of effort must be expended to achieve an adequate level of communication. If you have difficulty with communication now, it will only get more difficult.

- Set reasonable expectations. A church's expectations are based on past performance. Thus, one church may expect more than the other. Communicating reasonable expectations to both congregations before the merger will go a long way in helping the merger succeed.

- Determine the roles and positions for the pastors before the merger takes place. The attitudes, expectations, value systems, and leadership styles of the pastors are critical. If there are two pastors, one from each church, it is crucial that they work together well. Roles, duties, and personalities must be meshed before the merger takes place. When only one church has a pastor, the other church should look at the pastor as if they were considering him for their church alone. If the congregation would not be willing to call the pastor to their church, they should not merge with the other one.

- Clearly define where the buck stops. A church has a need for a clearly defined leader. When two pastors are involved, it is normal for most people to look to their pastor for leadership rather than to the other church's pastor.

- Develop an administration with one governing board, one staff, one treasury, one treasurer, and one budget.

- Move to a new location and into a new building together rather than having one church move into the building of another church.

- Make certain that leadership and ministry roles are filled with people from both churches. If leaders from only one church are used, good leaders from the other will move on to another church.

- Help those with concerns to understand and accept the merger. If leaders meet with and discuss the needs of people, they will help the merger be successful.

Questions to Ask and Answer

It must be recognized that people determine the success of a merger in differing ways. Some will look at what happens as a success, while others will see it as a failure. Those who define success in terms of unity will see it as a success even if most people leave. Those who define it in terms of numerical growth will see it as a failure. Before deciding to merge, each church should ask and answer each of the following questions, giving thought to how each impacts the potential success or failure of coming together.

1. What is the age of each church?
2. What crises have occurred at each church over the years?
3. What has been the growth patterns during the last ten years?
4. What are the ages of the neighborhoods?
5. How far do people drive to each church in terms of miles and time? What general directions do people drive to each church? Where do each church's worshipers live?
6. What are the pastoral strengths and weaknesses of each pastor? What complementation could there be? What potential job descriptions could there be? What would the working relationship be between staff? With whom would the buck stop?
7. What redundancies in staffing are there, and how would they be handled? How could staff be integrated?
8. What additional staff needs would need to be addressed?

9. What are the characteristics of each board, and how might they be integrated in the proposed merger?
10. What are each board's needs?
11. Is each board open to change?
12. What have been each church's most significant accomplishments over the last ten years?
13. What would each church want to preserve, avoid, and achieve?
14. What are the differences and similarities in terms of belief, doctrine, and tradition between the churches?
15. What are each congregation's attitudes toward growth and fruitfulness? Vision? Mission? Goals?
16. How does each church feel about the other congregation so far? What shared events can be started?
17. If the churches merge, how can the us-versus-them syndrome be avoided?
18. How does each congregation feel about the merger concept itself?
19. How would foreign missions be accomplished?
20. Are there any style issues that need to be addressed?
21. Should there be any conditions or safeguards established in case things don't work out?
22. What would happen with the money from the sale of property?
23. What percent of unhappy people would there be in each congregation, and how would they be handled?
24. What would the overall evangelistic vision be?
25. Is it feasible to relocate to a neutral site, property, or facility?
26. How would congregational members' roles dovetail?
27. How do the churches understand the general sequencing of the merger? What are the exact steps and procedures to be taken? What is the time line?
28. What is the length of commitment from the two pastors?

29. How long will it take members to get to know one another? Take time to court and fall in love, and get premerge counseling before signing the deal.
30. What happens when the usual visible objects of loyalty—a pastor, a building, a well-ordered church life—are removed? What is left for people to attach themselves to?

The Unspoken Issue

When two churches begin to think about merging, the first question they consider is whether they are theologically compatible. This is an important question, but it is a different issue that tends to doom most church mergers: culture.

Any church merger is doomed if there is no real effort beforehand to see if the two cultures have anything in common. Yet, church leaders too often regard cultural chemistry as a pesky detail that can be taken care of after the merger has taken place. This is a serious error. If the merger looks good but there are cultural problems, don't move ahead. The idea of fixing such problems later is a sure pathway to destruction. On the other hand, if two churches understand each other and their cultures mesh, people will say, "We can work out anything." If not, they will say, "We knew we couldn't trust those people."

The tiny intangibles that make up a church's personality, from styles of dress, to whether people and pastors are on a first name basis, to the number of committees, are not easily altered. Churches with clashing styles can end up living under the same roof but in perpetual disagreement. Neither church should impose its methods on the other. Rather, both together should seek to do everything better by building a new culture.

Appendix C

Recommended Reading

Anderson, Neil T., and Charles Mylander. *Setting Your Church Free: A Biblical Plan to Help Your Church*. Ventura, CA: Gospel Light, 1999.

Barna, George. *Turnaround Churches: How to Overcome Barriers to Growth and Bring New Life to an Established Church*. Ventura, CA: Regal Books, 1993.

Bennis, Warren G., and Burt Nanus. *Leaders: The Strategies for Taking Charge*. New York: Harper & Row, 1985.

Borden, Paul D. *Assaulting the Gates: Aiming All God's People at the Mission Field*. Nashville: Abingdon, 2009.

———. *Direct Hit: How Denominations Can Aim Congregations at the Mission Field*. Nashville: Abingdon, 2006.

———. *Hit the Bullseye: Aiming Real Leaders at the Mission Field*. Nashville: Abingdon, 2006.

Canfield, Jack. *The Success Principles: How to Get from Where You Are to Where You Want to Be*. New York: Collins, 2005.

Chand, Samuel R. *Ladder Shifts: New Realities, Rapid Change, Your Destiny*. Niles, IL: Mall Publishing, 2006.

Collins, James C. *Good to Great: Why Some Companies Make the Leap and Others Don't*. New York: Harper Business, 2001.

Crandall, Ron. *Turnaround and Beyond*. Nashville: Abingdon, 1995, 2008.

Dale, Robert D. *To Dream Again: How to Help Your Church Come Alive*. Nashville: Broadman, 1981.

Easum, Bill. *A Second Resurrection: Leading Your Congregation to New Life*. Nashville: Abingdon, 2007.

Eymann, Daniel C. "Turnaround Church Ministry: The Causes of Decline and the Changes Needed for Turnaround." DMin diss., Phoenix Seminary, Phoenix, AZ, 2011.

Finkin, Eugene F. *Successful Corporate Turnarounds: A Guide for Board Members, Financial Managers, Financial Institutions, and Other Creditors*. New York: Quorum Books, 1987.

Frazee, Randy, and Lyle E. Schaller. *The Comeback Congregation: New Life for a Troubled Ministry*. Nashville: Abingdon, 1995.

Gifford, Mary Louise. *The Turnaround Church: Inspiration and Tools for Life-Sustaining Change*. Herndon, VA: Alban Institute, 2009.

Gilbert, R., Jr. "Death by Merger." *The Christian Ministry* (July 1977): 30–32.

Hunter, George G., III. *Leading and Managing a Growing Church*. Nashville: Abingdon, 2000.

Kaiser, Walter C., Jr. *Quest for Renewal: Personal Revival in the Old Testament*. Chicago: Moody, 1986.

Kotter, John P. *Leading Change*. Boston: Harvard Business School Press, 1996.

Kouzes, James M., and Barry Z. Pozner. *The Leadership Challenge*. 4th ed. San Francisco: Jossey-Bass, 2007.

MacDonald, Gordon. "Clean Out the Sludge." *Leadership* (2005). www.christianitytoday.com/le/2005/fall/12.36.html.

McIntosh, Gary L. *Taking Your Church to the Next Level: What Got You Here Won't Get You There*. Grand Rapids: Baker, 2009.

McIntosh, Gary L., and R. Daniel Reeves. *Thriving Churches in the Twenty-First Century: Ten Life-giving Systems for Vibrant Ministry*. Grand Rapids: Kregel, 2006.

McMahan, Martin Alan. "Training Turn-around Leaders: Systemic Approaches to Reinstating Growth in Plateaued Churches." PhD diss., Fuller Theological Seminary, School of World Missions, Pasadena, CA, 1998.

Nixon, David F. *Leading the Comeback Church: Help Your Church Rebound from Decline*. Kansas City, MO: Beacon Hill, 2004.

Oaks, Fred. "Renewing Older Churches." *Leadership* (2005). www.christianitytoday.com/le/2005/fall/4.47.html.

Penfold, Gordon Everett. "Defining Characteristics of Turnaround Pastors among Evangelical Churches in the Rocky Mountain States." DMin thesis, Talbot School of Theology, Biola University, La Mirada, CA, 2011.

Rainer, Thom S. *Breakout Churches: Discover How to Make the Leap*. Grand Rapids: Zondervan, 2005.

Robinson, Anthony. *Transforming Congregational Culture*. Grand Rapids: Eerdmans, 2003.

Schaller, Lyle E. *44 Steps off the Plateau*. Nashville: Abingdon, 1993.

———. *A Mainline Turnaround: Strategies for Congregations and Denominations.* Nashville: Abingdon, 2005.

———. *The Small Church IS Different!* Nashville: Abingdon, 1982.

———. "To Merge or Not to Merge." *Net Results* (1991): 3–5.

Slatter, Stuart, David Lovett, and Laura Barlow. *Leading Corporate Turnaround: How Leaders Fix Troubled Companies.* San Francisco: Jossey-Bass, 2006.

Stetzer, Ed, and Mike Dodson. *Comeback Churches: How 300 Churches Turned Around and Yours Can Too.* Nashville: Broadman & Holman, 2009.

Thomas, Robert W. "Personality Characteristics of Effective Revitalization Pastors in Small, Passive Baptist General Conference Churches." DMin diss., Talbot School of Theology, Biola University, La Mirada, CA, 1989.

Tomberlin, Jim, and Warren Bird. *Better Together: Making Church Mergers Work.* San Francisco: Jossey-Bass, 2012.

Towns, Elmer L., C. Peter Wagner, and Thom S. Rainer. *The Everychurch Guide to Growth: How Any Plateaued Church Can Grow.* Nashville: Broadman & Holman, 1998.

Wagner, C. Peter. *Leading Your Church to Growth.* Ventura, CA: Regal Books, 1984.

———. *Your Church Can Grow.* Glendale, CA: Gospel Light, 1976.

Wilson, Gene A. *Revitalizing Congregational Life.* Ann Arbor, MI: University Microfilms, 1980.

Wood, Gene. *Leading Turnaround Churches.* St. Charles, IL: ChurchSmart, 2001.

Wood, Gene, and Daniel Harkavy. *Leading Turnaround Teams.* St. Charles, IL: ChurchSmart, 2004.

Youngblood, Duane E. *Making a Turnaround: Reversing Generational Curses.* Tarentum, PA: Word Association, 2003.

Notes

Chapter 1: See the Potential

1. Jerry Pence, "Church the Way It Ought to Be," *Mandate* (Winter 2003): 3.

Chapter 2: Commit to Lead

1. For further information on Ken Priddy's ministry, see the Ken Priddy Group, www.kenpriddy.com.

2. Terry Walling, "The Need for Hope," *Church Smart* 3, no. 4 (March 2000): 1.

3. I say generally because this simple two-question profile is not conclusive. The best results come from taking one of the well-designed and tested DISC personality instruments. However, I've found that answering these two questions usually pinpoints most people's basic personality type. For information on completing the full DISC profile, contact the author.

4. C. Peter Wagner, *Leading Your Church to Growth* (Ventura, CA: Regal Books, 1984), 97.

5. See dissertations by Robert Thomas and Gordon Penfold in appendix C for research on personality characteristics of revitalization leaders.

6. Howard F. Sugden and Warren W. Wiersbe, *Confident Pastoral Leadership* (Chicago: Moody, 1973), 9.

7. Robert W. Thomas, "Personality Characteristics of Effective Revitalization Pastors in Small, Passive Baptist General Conference Churches" (DMin diss., Talbot School of Theology, Biola University, 1989), 113.

8. John C. Maxwell, *Developing the Leader within You* (Nashville: Nelson, 1993), 1–13.

9. Chris Conrad, "Paying the Price When You Feel Like Selling Out," *Mandate* (Winter 2003): 10–11.

10. Thomas, "Personality Characteristics of Effective Revitalization Pastors," 112.

11. I heard Sam Chand state this at a leadership network conference sometime in 2008. For a full analysis of the place of pain in a leader's life see Samuel R. Chand, *Ladder Shifts: New Realities, Rapid Change, Your Destiny* (Niles, IL: Mall Publishing, 2006).

Chapter 3: Assess the Situation

1. Stephen Gray and Franklin Dumond, *Legacy Churches* (St. Charles, IL: ChurchSmart Resources, 2009).

2. Jon M. Van Dine, "Land Mines and Hand Grenades: Negotiating Hazardous Territory in the Declining Church," *Growing Churches* (July/August/September 1994): 11.

3. For further insight on what happens behind the curtain, see Gary L. McIntosh and R. Daniel Reeves, *Thriving Churches in the Twenty-First Century* (Grand Rapids: Kregel, 2006).

4. Ron Tovmassian, "Revitalization versus Reconstruction" (unpublished paper, Talbot School of Theology, La Mirada, CA, April 24, 2010), 3.

5. For a full description of how to lead a church in evaluation and planning, see Gary L. McIntosh, *Here Today, There Tomorrow* (Indianapolis: Wesleyan Publishing, 2010).

6. For consulting services, contact the author at http://churchgrowthnetwork.com/consulting or the Society for Church Consulting at www.churchconsultation.org.

Chapter 4: Learn the Principles

1. John C. Larue Jr., "Back from the Brink," *Your Church* (September/October 2006): 10.

2. Walter C. Kaiser Jr., *Quest for Renewal: Personal Revival in the Old Testament* (Chicago: Moody, 1986), 103.

3. For help in this area, see Neil T. Anderson and Charles Mylander, *Setting Your Church Free: A Biblical Plan to Help Your Church* (Ventura, CA: Gospel Light, 1999).

Chapter 6: Build a Coalition

1. Quoted in Stephanie Smith, "Peak Performance," *Success* (April 2010): 46.

2. Lyle E. Schaller, *Hey, That's Our Church* (Nashville: Abingdon, 1975), 93–96.

3. William M. Easum, "Warning! Turning a Church Around Is a Dangerous Calling," *Net Results* (September 1999): 21.

Chapter 7: Lift the Morale

1. George Barna, *User Friendly Churches: What Christians Need to Know about the Churches People Love to Go To* (Ventura, CA: Regal Books, 1991).

Chapter 8: Make Hard Decisions

1. "Humbled GM Files for Bankruptcy Protection," www.msnbc.msn.com/id/31030038.
2. Lyle Schaller, *The Win Arn Growth Report* (Pasadena, CA: Institute for American Church Growth, n.d.), 4.

Chapter 9: Refocus the Ministry

1. Barry Campbell, "Help a Church Move off the Plateau," *Growing Churches* (January/February/March 1992): 19.

Chapter 10: Equip for Change

1. This listing of adopter categories is adapted from Everett M. Rogers, *Diffusion of Innovations,* 5th ed. (New York: Free Press, 2003), 267–96.

Chapter 11: Deal with Resistance

1. Gene Wood, "Turning Your Church Around," *Mandate* (Winter 2003): 23.

Chapter 12: Stay the Course

1. Ron Kurtus, "Winston Churchill's Never Give In Speech of 1941," http://school-for-champions.com/speeches/churchill_never_give_in.htm.
2. Brian D. Bio, *Beyond Success: The Fifteen Secrets to Effective Leadership and Life Based on Legendary Coach John Wooden's Pyramid of Success* (New York: Berkley, 2001), xv–xvi.
3. Adapted from Jack Canfield, *The Success Principles* (New York: Collins, 2005), 175–76.
4. Ibid., 171.
5. Geoff Pound, "Jim Collins Asks Are You a Hedgehog or a Fox?" in *Stories for Speakers and Writers,* http://storiesforspeakers.blogspot.com/2008/09/jim-collins-asks-are-you-hedgehog-or.html.

Appendix B: Church Mergers

1. Anne B. Fisher, "How to Make a Merger Work," *Fortune* (January 24, 1994): 66.
2. Jim Tomberlin and Warren Bird, *Better Together: Making Church Mergers Work* (San Francisco: Jossey-Bass, 2012).

Gary L. McIntosh, DMin, PhD, is an internationally known author, speaker, consultant, and professor of Christian ministry and leadership at Talbot School of Theology, Biola University, located in La Mirada, California. He has written extensively in the field of pastoral ministry, leadership, generational studies, and church growth.

Dr. McIntosh received a BA in biblical studies from Colorado Christian University, an MDiv in pastoral studies from Western Conservative Baptist Seminary, a DMin in church growth studies from Fuller Theological Seminary, and a PhD in intercultural studies from Fuller's School of International Studies.

As president of the Church Growth Network, a church-consulting firm he founded in 1989, Dr. McIntosh has served over five thousand churches in eighty-three denominations throughout the United States and Canada. The 1995 and 1996 president of the American Society for Church Growth, he edited the *Journal of the American Society for Church Growth* for fourteen years. He currently edits *Growth Points*, a nationally read newsletter offering insights for ministry leaders in the United States and Canada. To interact with Dr. McIntosh on his blog, go to www.churchgrowthnetwork. com and click on blog.

Gary L. McIntosh speaks to numerous churches, nonprofit organizations, schools, and conventions each year. Services available include keynote presentations at major meetings, seminars and workshops, training courses, and ongoing consultation.

For a live presentation of the material found in *There's Hope for Your Church,* or to request a catalog of materials or other information on Dr. McIntosh's availability and ministry, contact:

Church Growth Network
PO Box 892589
Temecula, CA 92589-2589
951-506-3086
www.churchgrowthnetwork.com

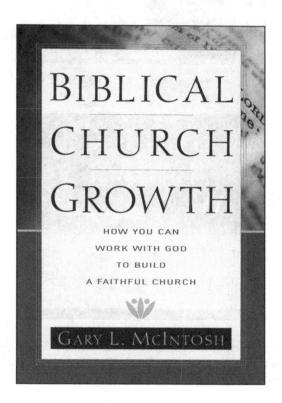

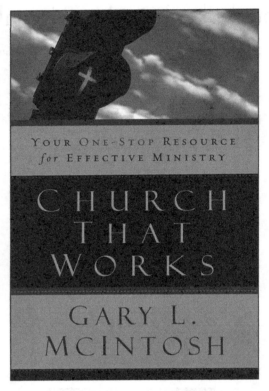

"Becoming a strong leader requires not only the cultivation of God-given gifts, but the ability to overcome negative factors. I recommend *Overcoming the Dark Side of Leadership*."

—John Maxwell, founder of INJOY

Successful leaders are deeply influenced by childhood experiences, which provide the motivation for their work and success as adults. Paradoxically, these experiences can also have a negative impact on their personal and professional lives. The "dark side of leadership" emerges when personal dysfunctions remain unaddressed. McIntosh and Rima offer a series of steps to help leaders take control of their dark side.

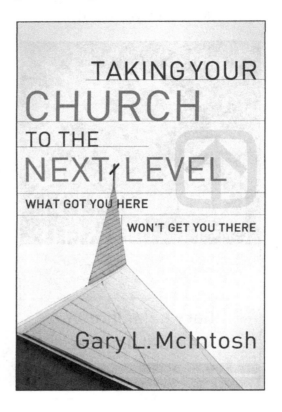